RECESSION CRISIS MANAGEMENT

Edited by

Rajib Lochan Panigrahy
M.A., PGDCA. MBA

Dr. Sudhansu Sekhar Nayak
Senior Lecturer
Deptt. of Commerce
R.N. College, Dura
Berhampur (Orissa)

&

Dr. Anil Kumar Sahu
M.B.A
Reader
Deptt. of Business Administration
Berhampur University
Berhampur (Orissa)

DISCOVERY PUBLISHING HOUSE PVT. LTD.
NEW DELHI-110 002

Published by:
Tilak Wasan

DISCOVERY PUBLISHING HOUSE PVT. LTD.
4831/24, Ansari Road, Prahlad Street
Darya Ganj, New Delhi-110002 (India)
Phone: +91-11-23279245, 43764432
Fax: +91-11-23253475
E-mail: parul.wasan@gmail.com
discoverypublishinghouse@gmail.com
info@discoverypublishinggroup.com
web: www.discoverypublishinggroup.com

***First Edition:* 2011**
ISBN: 978-81-8356-820-3

Recession Crisis Management

Printed at:
Shree Balaji Art Press
Delhi

Preface

Recession can be defined as a slowing down of the activity in an economy. A decline in the GDP growth of a country over two or more consecutive quarters of a year in a country is the hallmark of recession. There is consensus that recession is a normal part of a business cycle and it would last between 6 to 12 months. Researchers state that recession is the period between when business activity after reaching a peak starts to fall and when it ultimately reaches bottom. Less spending by consumers due to lack of faith in the country is the cardinal feature of recession. Less spending results in a decline in demand for products followed cuts in production, rise in levels of unemployment and eventually decline in levels of GDP in a country. First growing sectors in India like IT sector have witnessed a moderate decline in growth rate. There was a recessive squeeze on business profits which has picked up demand for upper real estate and demand for durable households declined.

The book contains 13 articles of research on the recent developments and deteriorations of organisational, economic slowdowns and affects in the time of global recession period on financial crisis, HR issues at Merger and Acquisition, affects on Marketing, customer's attitude of buying FMCG and consumer durables, Internet banking opportunities and its response-usage by bank executives, E-commerce and M-Commerce, NPA management of PSU Banks, higher education opportunities to foreign participants, SME sector, etc. The themes are described by the eminent researchers from different reputed colleges and universities mainly from the Faculties of Management, Economics and Commerce.

They have attempted their level best and contributed to this volume by elaborating their research topics to make the book self-sufficient. We are very much grateful to the paper contributors and the publisher for their kind heartedness to complete the volume. Otherwise this volume may see the limelight.

Authors

Contents

Contributors

1. *Dr. Kabita Kumari Sahu,* Lecturer in Economics, North Orissa University, Baripada, Orissa.
2. *Snigdha Mohapatra,* Faculty HR Placement Coordinator INC, (now IIPS) Cuttack, Orissa
3. *Manit Mis*hra Assistant Professor and Dean (Student Welfare) at DRIEMS Business School, Cuttack, Orissa.
4. *Dr. Shirish R. Kulkarni,* Reader, Deptt. of Accounting and Financial Management, Faculty of Commerce, The M.S. University of Baroda, Sayajigunj, Vadodara, Gujara.
5. *Chirag P. Surti,* Co-author, Research Student, Dept. of Accounting and Financial Management, Faculty of Commerce, The M.S. University of Baroda, Sayajigunj, Vadodara, Gujarat.
6. *Rajesh D. Shelke,* Assistant Professor, Department of Agricultural Economics and Statistics, College of Agriculture, Latur, Marathwada Agricultural University, Parbhani, Maharashtra.
7. *Dr. R.K.Uppal,* Principal Investigator, University Grants Commission Sponsored Major Research Project, D.A.V College, Malout-152107, Punjab.
8. *Poonam Rani,* Project Fellow, University Grant Commission Sponsored Major Research Project, D.A.V. College, Malout-152107, Punjab.
9. *Manoranjan Dash,* Lecturer, Institute of Business and Computer Studies, Siksha O Anusandhan University,

Ghatikia, Kalinga Nagar, SUM Hospital Road, Bhubaneswar-3

10. *Dr. A. Abdul Raheem,* S.S. Lecturer in Economics, The New College, Chennai-14
11. *Dr. T.Muthiyen,* S.S. Lecturer in Economics, The New College, Chennai-14
12. *Subhrabala Behera,* Ph.D Scholar (Political Science), Utkal University, Bhubaneswar, Orissa
13. *Dr. B. Eswar Rao Pattnaik,* Sr. Reader in Economics, S.B.R.G. Women's College, Berhampur.
14. *Dr. Sudhansu Sekhar Nayak,* Sr. Faculty in Commerce, R.N. College, Dura, Berhampur
15. *Dr. Sudhakar Patra,* Reader in Economics, Ravenshaw University, Cuttack, Orissa
16. *Prabin Kumar Padhy,* Head, Department of Management, Gayatri Institute of Science and Technology, Berhmapur, Orissa.
17. *Dr. S.K. Choudhury,* Faculty Member, Alphia Institute of Business Management, Bhubaneswar, Orissa
18. *Dr. P.C. Mahapatra,* Reader in Commerce, Maharsi College of Natural Law, Bhubaneswar, Orissa.
19. *Prof. K.R. Swain,* Sr. Faculty, IPSAR 'B' School, Cuttack, Orissa

CHAPTER 1

Global Financial Crisis and India's Response

—DR. KABITA KUMARI SAHU

ABSTRACT

The objective of this paper to analyse the origin, nature and impact of financial crisis started in late 2008 with its epicenter in the financial system of USA. The explosive growth of USA during last three decades due to deregulation, technological innovation, growing international mobility of capital and unsustained path of growth are the factors behind economic meltdown of USA. Most of the advanced countries are already in the grip of recession and the economic outlook for the developing countries including India is detoriating rapidly. The feeling production, reduction in volume of trade, joblessness and rise in international food prices aggravated the crisis in many countries. The Government of India adopted several stimulus packages and pragmatic policy with additional spending on infrastructure and tax concessions to lessen the adverse effects of global meltdown. The Reserve Bank of India moved quickly to improve liquidity capital and to reduce the risk of investment. The drop in real estate and stock prices and job cuts in the employment market, particularly in export oriented industries are the backwash effects of global financial crisis. The falling rupee against dollar, liquidity and confidence are the main problems of crisis in Indian Financial system.

In this context this paper highlights the impact and spread of crisis on Indian economy through financial real and confidence channels. The monetary policy responses and fiscal stimulus of government are analysed with impact on various sectors. Indian economy has several advantages over other countries due to comfortable reserve position, sound and healthy banking system, priority sector lending and social safety net programmes in addressing the adverse impact of global economic crisis. Hence, this paper presents detailed analysis of degree and spread of global economic crisis with its impact on Indian Economy and responses to mitigate adverse impact on real and financial sectors of our country.

Introduction

Recession is an economic situation of business cycle contraction and slowdown in economic activities which leads to fall in production, employment, household income, investment, capacity utilisation, wholesale-retail sales, trade and business profit. A global recession is a period of global economic slowdown. According to IMF, global economic growth of 3 point or less is equivalent to a global recession. Negative real economic growth for atleast two quarters (six months) or 1.5 per cent rise in unemployment withen 12 months can be described as a situation of global recession. The global nature of the current crisis has been unprecedented as several advanced countries have simultaneously witnessed declines in house and equity prices as well as difficulty in their credit markets. The current crisis is accompanied with severe credit crunches resulting output losses and decline in consumption, investment and employment. A national recession is identified by two quarters of decline in productivity but global recession is more difficult to define. IMF estimates that global recession seems to occur over a cycle lasting 8 to 10 years.

The global economy is facing unprecedented crisis with falling production and job cuts. The advanced countries are in the grip of recession and the developing countries like India has received the shock and uncertainties which has created pessimism in production sector. The crisis in India is largly an imported one, primarily via the trade and investment routes (Subarao, 2009). The present crisis is the result of an uneven and unsustainable global growth pattern emerging since 2000. Strong consumer demand, easy credit, high rate of investment demand and strong export growth of many countries led to such unbalanced growth pattern. Increasing financial deregulation, flurry of new financial instrument, mortgage backed securities, collateral debt obligations, credit default swap encouraged massive accumulation of financial asset slowly leading to financial crisis. This crisis is mainly due to deficiencies in the regulatory and supervisory framework of financial markets. The international trade is contracting and growth of merchandise trade decelerated to 4 per cent. In 2009, this growth may decline by 9 per cent (B.P. Mathur, 2009). So, global economic recession has affected directly to the financial sector and indirectly to the real sector of many countries.

Attributes and Origin of Global Financial Crisis

Several advanced countries have simultaneously witnessed declines in equity prices and difficulties in their credit markets towards late 2008. The present global crisis is in the form of a recession which lasts on an average for one year with substantial variation with shortest recession for two quarters and the longest thirteen quarters (Claessens et al., 2008). The major financial firm crisis started with Lehman Brothers which filed for bankrupting after the Federal Reserve Bank declined to participate in creating a financial support facility on 14th September 2008. There was extreme instability in global stock markets with dramatic drops in market values of shares. American International Group (AIG) suffered a liquidity crisis on 16th September 2008 which became insolvent and suspended dividends to previously issued firms. The sub-prime mortgage crisis reached a critical stage in

September 2008 which contracted liquidity in global credit markets and insolvency threats to investment banks and other institutions. The stock market crash and rise in reverse balances from banks in the federal reserve system of USA created a financial panic around the world. This financial crisis percolated to other countries and also to India through financial channels Indian stock market suffered a crisis with high instability of equity prices. So, the global financial crisis of 2008-09 which became prominently visible in September 2008 with the failure, merger and conservatorship of several large United States based financial firms. The failure of large financial institutions of USA rapidly evolved into a global economic crisis resulting in a number of European bank failures and declines in various stock indexes. The crisis led to a liquidity problem and the deliveraging of financial institutions in Europe and USA which further accelerated the liquidity crisis and decrease in international shipping and commerce. The crisis was triggered by the sub-prime mortgage crisis and became an acute phase of the financial crisis. According to the World Economic Outlook of IMF the world economy is facing the major downturn and the most dangerous shock since 1930. It expects global growth due to recession to come down to 3 per cent by the end of 2009. According to David H. Wang any global growth rate under 2.0 per cent is tantamount to a recession. Europe's largest economy of Germany contracted by 0.5 per cent in 2008. Growing deficits of USA were financed by increasing trade surpluses by China, Japan and other countries which had accumulated large foreign exchange reserves. The international trade decelerated 4 per cent after financial crisis which was 6 per cent between 1990 to 2006. The WTO predicted that the volume of global merchandise trade would shrink by 9 per cent in 2009.

Due to global financial crisis, there has been a return to Keynesianism even in the capitalist countries with the state taking a native role in stimulating economic activity and boosting demand. Marx's prediction of periodic booms and busts in capitalistic economies appears to be true due to the present global financial crisis.

Aftermath of Crisis and Impact on Developing Countries

A financial crisis and recession creates a psychology of fear and panic among the investors and businessmen which has serious social and economic cosequences.The global down turn in the financial system did not affect the banking system of developing countries directly but risk and recession emerged from other channels. The international investors pooled back resources from the developing countries as a part of deleveraging process of financial institutions. The volatility of the foreign exchange markets has increased substantially by deepening the financial crisis. The growth rate of many developing countries declined to less than 6 per cent against 7 per cent for last several years. The growth in these economies is decelerating due to weakening of export demand, lower commodity prices and a decline in investment flow to the region. The rise in prices of foodgrains in international market caused untold sufferings in developing countries which are dependent on food imports. The tightening access to credit and weaker growth will cut into public revenues to meet the necessary investment into education, health and other social needs. The global financial crisis is hitting developing countries of South Asia when they are already reeling from the adverse effects of a severe terms of trade shocks. The adverse effects of this terms of trade shocks have been substantial and reflected in a slowdown of growth, worsening in macroeconomic balances and huge inflationary pressures. The global financial crisis will adversely affect the export, home remittances and domestic investment in developing countries.

Contagion Impact on Indian Economy

Indian economy was growing at 8 to 9 per cent before 2008 and the growth rate has slowed down to around 6 per cent. The stock market in India has lost 50 per cent of its value and the rupee has lost 20 per cent of its value in terms of dollar. There has been huge job losses in all the sectors of the economy and particularly export oriented industries like textile, diamond cutting and polishing. Even in high profile IT sector, fresh recruitment and job creation has stopped after the global crisis. The Government of India adopted several stimulus packages and pragmatic economic policies to save the economy from global meltdown.

Indian economy has been less hit by the crisis because the Indian banking system has had no direct exposure to the sub prime mortgage assets of failed institutions. Due to very limited off balance sheet activities, Indian banks continue to remain safe and healthy. Secondly India's growth has been driven predominantly by domestic consumption and investment. External demand accounts for less than 15 per cent of our GDP. Hence Indian Economy is less affected due to limited depends on external demand in spite of a global down turn. The effects of global crisis on our economy can be understood from fallowing facts:

(*i*) The financial integration of India with the world is very deep along with trade globalisation. The ratio of total external transaction to GDP has increased more than double from 46.8 per cent in 1997-98 to 117.4 per cent in 2007-08 (*D. Subarao,* 2009)

(*ii*) India's integration into the world economy in post reform period has been rapid and India's trend as proportion of GDP increased from 21.2 per cent in 1997-98 to 37.4 per cent in 2007-08.

(*iii*) The share of investment in GDP increased by 11 per cent during 2003-08. The foreign investors were willing to take risk and provide funds at lower costs due to India's growth potential.

Hence, India has been hit by the crisis due to rapid and growing integration into the global economy. The global economic crisis has spread to India through the real channel, financial channel and confidence channel. The money market, credit market and equity market came under pressure due to shifting of the credit demand by the Indian banks and corporates to the domestic banking sector. The substitution of foreign financing by the domestic financing pressurised money and credit markets in India.

Declining demand for experts due to global crisis affected domestic economy through the real channel. Service export growth slowed down and remittances from migrant workers decreased affected the Indian economy. The Indian banks became cautious about lending to avoid risk which affected the economy through confidence channel. So, global crisis adversely affected domestic output, employment through external shocks and domestic vulnerabilities. Effects on financial sector, real sector and macro economic balances are stated below :

(i) Financial Sector Effects : The effects of global crisis on financial sector depends on macroeconomic performances, health of banking system and exposure to foreign capital markets. India is relatively more exposed to the contagion effects of global financial markets through adverse effects on capital flows and direct foreign investment. There has been significant losses in the stock markets and reduction in the flow of foreign capital. These risks are addressed by India by prudent foreign debt management, high saving rate and pro-active monetary policy management to stabilise the financial sector. The Reserve Bank responded by providing extra liquidity to the financial sector and by raising the limit on private foreign borrowing.

(ii) The real sector effects: The real sector effects of global crisis work through export, import, remittances and investment. The crisis has lowered the export prospects of India by a sharp slowdown in demand particularly in service sector. The export of textile and garment sector is worst affected by global recession. The imports observed downward trend especially in food and fuel. The remittances from OECD countries have reduced substantially after the crisis. The foreign direct investment and domestic investment has slowed down due to risk and uncertainties.

(iii) Effects on Macroeconomic Balances: The adverse terms of trade and falling commodity prices have resulted lower demand and macroeconomic imbalances. Inflation has been coming down in our country in spite of rising food prices. The fiscal picture is likely to improve due to lower subsidies.

India's Response and Policy Measures

Expansionary macroeconomic policies are generally adopted by government to take remedial measures. The Government and Reserve Bank of India responded quickly to reduce the adverse impact of global economic crisis on Indian economy in close co-ordination and consultation. The fiscal stimulus and monetary accommodation helped to face the challenges of crisis strongly in spite of uncertain and unsettle global financial market. The important policies are as follows :

(*i*) Government of India sanctioned Rs 20,000 crores more as non-plan expenditure in first phase.

(*ii*) All State Governments were permitted to raise Rs. 20,000 crores more loan.

(*iii*) The Reserve Bank brought down CRR to 5 per cent and REPO rate to 4 per cent.

(*iv*) All nationalised banks were supplied additional capital to the extent of Rs. 20,000 crores.

(*v*) Power sector, textile industry, steel industry, cement industry were given special incentives.

(*vi*) The Reserve Bank tried to keep the domestic money and credit markets to function normally without any liquidity stress. The RBI maintained comfortable rupee liquidity position, augmented foreign exchange liquidity and continued credit delivery by reducing interest rate aggressively.

(*vii*) The Government of India extended fiscal stimulus in the form of additional public spending, particularly capital expenditure, government guaranteed funds for infrastructure, reduction in indirect taxes and additional support to exporters.

(*viii*) The loan waiver package for farmers and salary increases for government employees stimulated domestic demand to face the crisis.

Conclusion

The origin of economic crisis are general and common around the world but it affected different countries differently. In developed countries the crisis spread from the financial sector to the real sector but in developing countries the transmission of external crisis has been form the real sector to the financial sector. The policy response in India has been to arrest moderation in economic growth. The service sector slowed down mainly in construction, transport, communication and trade. The exports declined during October-December 2008 and thereafter in absolute terms after seven years of continuous growth. The industrial production has shown negative growth during 2008-09 and demand for bank credit declined in spite of comfortable liquidity position. The impact of global crisis has less impact on India due to sound, healthy and well-regulated banking system of our country. The comfortable reserve position of Indian banks provide confidence to foreign investors. Institutional credit for agriculture remain unaffected and loan waiving policy saved the agriculture sector and partly from crisis. Hence, the poor and vulnerable groups of people are protected from adverse impact of global crisis due to extensive programmes in social sector.

The policy makers all over the world and India are trying to find out a solution to the cement crisis and looking for the best economic model to build a stable economy. Fiscal stimulus from Government of India is necessary to boost the domestic consumption and expansion of health, education and other social indicators. The government investment in infrastructure, acceleration of financial development, reforms in public enterprise can help in addressing the crisis. The banking system and industrial infrastructure in the country should be strengthened. Government should increase it's spending to create more jobs in manufacturing sector. Direct foreign investment should be channalised more to productive activities. It is high time for policy makers to act swiftly and decisively to undertake the necessary measures at both national and global levels to meet the challenges of crisis.

REFERENCES

1. Claessens S., Kose M. A and Terrones M. E. (2008) Global Financial Crisis: How Long? How deep? *http://www.voxue.org/index.php.*
2. Islam M. S. (2008) : South Asia's Inflation Challenges, *ISAS Insights,* No. 26, Singapore, 28, March.
3. Lahiri, A. (2009) : Indian Financial Reforms : National Priorities Amidst an International Crisis. *Sir Purushotamadas Thakurdas Memorial Lecture,* Mumbai.
4. Mathur, B.P. (2009) : Global Economic Crisis : Lessons for India, *Mainstream,* Volume—XLVII, No. 25.
5. Nachane, D.M. (2007) : Liberalisation of the Capital Account : Perils and Possible Safeguards. *Economic and Political Weekly,* Vol. XLII, No. 36, Sept. 8-14, pp. 3633-3643.
6. National Commission for Enterprises in the Unorganised Sector (NCEUS) (Nov. 2008) : The Global Economic Crisis and the Informal Economy in India, Government of India.
7. Planning Commission, Government of India (2008) : Eleventh Five Year Plan, Vol. III.
8. Rediff.com.news(2008) : How the Global Financial Crisis Affect India.
9. Subarao, D. (2009) : The Global Economic Crisis and Challenges for the Asian Economy in a Changing World, *Speech delivered at the Symposium Tokyo* 18-February.
10. Sung hoon Cho (2007) : Financial Institutions and Markets, *Korea's Economic*, Vol. 23.
11. *The Economist* (2008) : The Decoupling Debate, 6th March.
12. United Nations (2009) : World Economic Situation and Prospects, New York.
13. World Bank (2008) : *Global Financial Crisis—Implications for South Asian Regions,* 21st October.

CHAPTER **2**

HR Issues at Merger and Acquisitions *A Case Study on Standard Chartered Wealth Managers*

—MS. SNIGDHA MOHAPATRA

Key Words

Merger and Acquisition (M&A), Restructuring, Standard Chartered Wealth Managers.

Introduction

Growth continues to be the most dominant entity in the mind and strategy of any CEO. To increase the value of the organisation the management needs to take care from each aspect, starting from stockholder's perception to the intension of the 4th grade employees. In the modern world with the advent of globalisation, liberalisation and privatisation it is Merger and Acquisition (M&A) that is living and leading everyone's eyes and views. M&A is the concept of buying, selling and combining of different business units that can aid, finance, or help a growing company in a given industry grow rapidly without having to create another business entity (*Wikipaedia*). This became the most favoured method of achieving growth targets and appeasing key stakeholders vigilant in their goal to increase shareholders value (*Jarrod McDonald, Max Coulthard, and Paul de Lange*). The corporate strategy to grow is expected to be fulfilled by M&A

only then when there is a proper alignment of both the strategies. It is found that one in three CEO interviewed had a clear strategic rationale for the M&A for their company's long term financial future (*Jarrod McDonald, Max Coulthard, and Paul de Lange*). Resource sites that India itself had undergone 1400 M&A worth of $59 billion.

Marriages not always made in heaven, it is more like two mind sets who have never dated, and now are thrown together because of the wishes of stockholders or boards over whom they have had no control (*Ethan A. Winning).* Failures to M&A are many. It is the initial plan, due diligence and integration that to be taken care so to ripe the fruits of M&A. Research by *Bain&Company* suggests that around 70 per cent of mergers fail to create meaningful shareholder value, often because the combined organisation has been unable to integrate quickly and achieve the rapid capture of identified synergies. Often M&A had emphasised on the financial adjustment overlooking the human resource part that carries the responsibility to achieve the target goal. M&A represent one of the greatest challenge a human resources department can face (*Neil Davey*). The HR department is expected to remain ready with the ideas to align and accomplish the goals of both companies' employees. *Billingham* explains this as a period when the capability and capacity of the HR function are most severely tested. The HR division is to get collectively the vision, skills, incentive, resources and action plan so to make the change acceptable and profitable from each point of view. As stated by *Ambrose* it is a proportionate mixture of vision, skills, incentive, resources and action plan that can make the change inevitable in any organisation.

The need of a better balance mechanism is the requirement of any HR to lead a successful M&A activity. The balance mechanism is a process to reach a desirable point between opposite forces. The advent of M&A expects the organisation to stand at the higher and wider financial position while the opposite track is maximum employee turnover to resist the change that takes place. To achieve the success the M&A company needs to identify the way out to balance both productivity and satisfaction of its employees. Time and resources required to implement plans while still continuing the usual business is the biggest challenge as stated by *2005 PwC Deal Confidence Survey*. The change resistant is wider in the very stage that makes the most efficient even to perform the worst. The present situation obviously demands a tool that can help the company both to prosper with productivity. That tool will show the way ahead to have control over the throughout development of the total in consideration to both employee and the organisation.

Inadequate knowledge about resource availability and lack of proper communication of the goal achievement path makes the situation worse even. People expects downsising through retrenchment and is more skeptical about their position *(K. Mallikarjun)*. Proper communication about the post and position helps all the staff members, no matter a supervisor or a medium level manager to come out of that dilemma. Staff restructuring is required to align staff roles with programmes and mission of the organisation. Reviewing the designation and power, reorienting the new industrial relation with revision of management style becomes the demand for post M&A *(K. Mallikarjun)*. Restructuring the positions inside the organisation means allocating the best responsibility to that same employee who can not only achieve that but also can have control over that. Restructuring is defined as changing the very outlook of the organisation in order to achieve the set vision.

UTI Securities, set up in 1994, has grown from an institutional brokerage house to a full-fledged financial intermediary having nationwide presence to serve a wide range of clients. The company has noteworthy presence in institutional and retail broking, online trading (www.usectrade.com), depository services, portfolio management services, equities research, merchant banking, fixed income securities, and distribution of financial products, among others. Securities Trading Corporation of India is one of the leading bond houses in the country. Securities Trading Corporation of India (STCI) has acquired broking and investment firm UTI Securities Ltd, for Rs 265 crore *(The Hindu Businessline)*. According to sources, there were about 10 bidders including Standard Chartered Bank. Standard Chartered Bank is took over 49 per cent stake in UTI Securities from the Securities Trading Corporation of India (STCI) for around Rs 140 crore in the month of May, 2007 (*The Economic Times*). Standard Chartered Private Bank has been named the "Global Best Private Bank" by Euromoney (*The Economic Times*). This bank with its 150 years of banking experience is experimenting at Indian laboratory to achieve the same acceptance and dominance as it owes in the global scenario on the name *'Standard Chartered Wealth Managers'*.

The present researcher is trying to find out the effort made by Standard Chartered Wealth Managers to come up successful at M&A with a simultaneous effort to add some suggestions for a fruitful achievement.

Objectives of the Study

The total world including developing countries like India is emphasising on M&A as a solution to their thirst of wide coverage and expansion. M&A seems to have failed many a times with the root cause at Human Resource. Therefore the study aims to find out:

1. The problems Standard Chartered Wealth Managers is expected to face after M&A from HR point of view;
2. The restructuring suggestions for Standard Chartered Wealth Managers to overcome the problems associated with HR.

Research Methodology

The research is based upon both primary and secondary data collected from different sources. The researcher aims at finding out the HR related problems that Standard Chartered Wealth Managers is undergoing through *personal interview* with specific open-ended questions. The research area is confined to the Bhubaneswar branch as per the convenience of the researcher. Researcher has to randomly select five manager level employees and ten executive level employees for personal interview. The sample size has been made small intentionally to justify the analysis process. Answers to open ended questions are to be analysed with the findings of the previous collected secondary data from different references like books, magazine, journals and Internet.

The second question is to be answered on the basis of secondary data collected from wide search at books, magazines, journals and internet.

Results

The primary data collected in the due course reveals that Standard Chartered Wealth Managers is undergoing following problems either already exposed or yet to be disclosed and felt by the organisation is:

First of all employees irrespective of their designation are dubious about *who is the leader*. Whether this is the rule and regulation that is followed to date is to be ruling tomorrow or not is the basic question in everyone's view.

Second is *identification of key people* inside the organisation and developing strategy for their *retention*. Each employee is doubtful about his/her immediate reporting authorities' position.

Supplying to the second point each employee is in a dilemma of his/her *presence requirement*. The question is to leave the organisation before he/she is asked to do so or to swim along the flow to survive in the organisation.

The last but not the least problem being highlighted is that employees are very much dissatisfied about the *working environment* that they are in, as it is drastically different to earlier. The work pressure and the authority divisions to pass the order are aggravating the problems articulated with work culture.

The employees of the organisation is still not sure about the name their merged organisation is carrying and is yet to be accompanied to the name Standard Chartered Wealth Managers. In this context answering to the second objective to find out solution at Standard Chartered Wealth Managers there is a clear-cut view to adopt staff restructuring *i.e.* identifying and defining the each employee's position and responsibility. The secondary data reveals that to avoid the skeptical eyes and views of employees' in M&A company's staff repositioning is the classic but up-to-date solution.

Interpretation

The foremost trouble is lack of head or leader identification is prevailing at Standard Chartered Wealth Managers. Change is the widely constant feature that use to generate resistance no matter where it is been introduced. Employees feel their immediate surrounding being confused as there are two companies together. In case of a clear acquisition people get confused about whether the existing leader is still ruling or it is the leader from the acquisition group. The situation is made even worse because of lack of lucidity in communication (*Nasha Fitter*). Lack of knowledge about actual leader creates havoc in the organisation.

Employees are not very sure about who is having the pressure to success and plays on their wild cards. They use to put their own perception into work. The immediate boss is a common position to talk about and the same happens at M&A. The perception says there is no perfect work distribution along the lines and so people are in stress and they will leave. This is the reason behind everyone's consideration to locate the key people and think for their retention. People perceive that what they feel. The underling cause is employees are not very sure about their position. They could not find the right path to travel and tries to hit in dark. As people are aware of downsizing they consider it indirectly by citing the example of their immediate supervisors.

Working environment irrespective of all the bits and pieces cited above is the main problem identified by the employees. Research says M&A fails to attend its all round success when employees are not aligned with the goal of the organisation (*Geroge Wright*). The first and foremost role of HR lies at communicating perfectly the goal mean to be achieved and the very process to achieve so (*David Billingham*). The work pressure being transferred from time to target put people in trouble. Proper communication and implication leads to a better position for employees to identify the very work structure. Thus staff restructuring and identifying the role is a better solution to all these existing problems. Restructuring is a bare necessity to come out of responsibility confusion (*Nigel Perks*). Breaking up the ice is hard to do but once started travels the entire sphere of success. The organisation need to understand where to put the change. If else the organisation is reviving its power structure it is to be done openly and to be communicated properly. Finding out the structure is difficult but a HR division can perform the task as well by identifying the objective of each department to be achieved in collaboration to the responsibilities the existing employees have well incorporated. Employees can be motivated to apply and compete for different positions to have a smooth staff restructuring. Restructuring will make the progress not only clear rather will make it totally visible and attainable to the employees (*Jarrod Mc Dolland, Max Coulthard and Paul De Lange*).

Conclusion

"It is the people STUPID" quoted by Ann Pomeroy who decides the fate of the organisation. Give them a reason to believe they will think of the cause why it is given but give them a position they will justify the position by their deed.

This clearly state the role of power restructuring or staff restructuring to enjoy the ripen fruit of M&A.

REFERENCES

1. Billingham, D. (2002), *"HR and We at Organisation",* Human Resource Management, 152-154.
2. Chhabra, T.N. (2005), *"Human Resource Management—Concepts and Issues",* 5th ed, Dhanapati Rai & Co. (P) Ltd.
3. Jarrod Mc. C. Max, and Lange D.P. (2003), *"Planning for a Successful Merger and Acquisition",* Effective Management, 13-22.
4. Perks, N. (2008), *"Making Mergers Meaningful",* GDS Publishing Ltd.
5. Rao, V.S.P. and Rao, S. (1990), *"Personal/Human Resource* Management, Texts, Cases and Games", 5th ed, Konark Publishers Pvt. Ltd.
6. Robbins, S.P. (2005), *"Organisational Change",* 11th ed. Printice Hall India Publication.
7. Wright, G. (2008), *"M&A the Path of Success If You Want to Achieve",* Finance Management and People, Vol. 2, 7-12.

CHAPTER 3

Materialism
Marketer's Key Ally Against Downturn

—MANIT MISHRA

ABSTRACT

The research paper attempts to delve deep into the consumer psyche to unearth remedies to the present recessionary trend. The paper puts forward the argument that merely making cosmetic changes in the marketing mix elements may not be the best option available to the marketer in the times of economic downturn. A tactical modification in the marketing mix elements, though essential, would be useless unless it is able to arouse consumer's materialistic tendencies. The paper goes on to deliberate on the construct materialism from the Indian perspectives, highlighting the existence of divergent schools of thought. The paper elucidates upon the very strong relationship between materialism and marketing, as bought out by prior research on the subject. The research paper finally culminates with a commentary on the interplay between morality, materialism and marketing.

Introduction

Case 1 : During the economic depression of 1907 in USA, William Wrigley Jr. the founder of Wrigley—the largest gum manufacturing company in the world—did something truly iconoclastic. Most of the companies reduced their costs owing to the downturn. However, Wrigley trusted his instincts and went against the accepted logic. In the midst of the financial frenzy, he could see the tremendous scope for advertising. Since other companies were cutting down on the communication budget, Wrigley seized the opportunity to advertise. He pumped in a huge US $250,000 so as to carry out a massive advertising campaign during that great depression in 1907. His efforts paid off and by 1910, Wrigley's Spearmint had become the most popular brand of chewing gum (*O'Neil 2004, p. 78*).

Analysis: Overtly, there seems to be two reasons for the success of William Wrigley. Firstly, because of a lack in demand, he was able to procure advertising space at cheaper rates and therefore, could carry out greater amount of promotion for a comparatively lesser budget. Secondly, since companies reduced their emphasis on advertising, Wrigley could communicate without being affected by clutter. It had customer's undivided attention.

Case 2: Kishore Biyani promoted Pantaloons Retail's same store sales during April 2009 in the lifestyle segment grew by 6.03 per cent to Rs. 119.53 crore. The highest growth in last 6 months, however, was achieved in January 2009 – at the height of consumer confidence breakdown—when sales increased by 12.05 per cent over the previous month. In absolute terms, lifestyle retailing has grown by 18.1 per cent during the period of November, 2008-April, 2009 to reach Rs. 135.81 crore (Business Standard, 14 May 2009).

Analysis: Kishore Biyani could achieve the impossible in these turbulent times since in January and February; Pantaloon's discount offer removed the difference between lifestyle products and value products. It was a clever strategy which allowed customers to fulfill their long cherished desires, at a lesser price, since even during an economic downturn, people do not stop consuming.

The two incidents discussed above are separated by a chronological gap of more than 100 years. They are also totally unrelated in terms of market dynamics, geographic locations and demographic characteristics. Another differentiating factor being, while William Wrigley Jr. was able to strengthen his position using *'promotion'* as a tool, Kishore Biyani did the same thing by using 'price' as the tool.

However, there is one underlying aspect, which unites these two seemingly incongruent measures by two different visionary strategists who happen to be market leaders in their own areas of activity. They successfully beat the low consumer confidence by looking beyond the black-and-white picture of recession and found ways to make the customer buy their respective products. They were able to arouse the apparently dormant human tendency of possession and consumption beyond what is necessary for existence. The present author strongly believes that the solution to beating recession does not lie in making cosmetic changes in the marketing mix of a company, but in making such subtle changes so as to make an impact on the consumer's psyche and arouse his tendency to derive satisfaction out of possession and consumption of material objects. In other words, even in the most trying times people do consume and therefore, marketer can successfully beat downturn if he is able to utilise the marketing mix elements to ignite the ambers of materialistic tendencies among the consumers.

Materialism—Indian Framework

The concepts of materialism, as an inherent constituent of lifestyle has been a profoundly dialectic construct. The issue has been of interest to a range of *homosapiens*—from the dilettante who have dabbled in its aura to the prophets whose homilies have castigated it as a source of retrogression towards spiritual bankruptcy. Materialism is indeed an eclectic notion which finds a mention in an entire gamut of disciplines. The bouquets and brickbats notwithstanding, the issue is a livewire and deserve investigation, more so in the backdrop of the current dismal economic scenario.

To appreciate the construct of materialism fully, it is imperative to understand the relevance of materialism in Indian culture from theological, philosophical and social perspectives. The coexistence of contradictory schools of thought on materialism for last 2,500 years and ensuing dialectics needs to be recognised and elucidated upon.

In Indian culture, materialism has been a widely debated issue with both proposing and opposing schools of thought. However, the oral tradition of passing on knowledge from one generation to another may have resulted in poor documentary evidence. Chatterjee and Datta (1984) explained that "though materialism in some form or other has always been present in India, and occasional references are found in the *Vedas*, the Buddhist literature, the epics as well as in the later philosophical works, we do not find any systematic work on materialism, nor any organised school of followers as the other philosophical schools possess. But almost every work of the other schools states, for refutation, the materialistic views. Our knowledge of Indian materialism is chiefly based on these".

The significance of materialism in Indian culture can not be fully imbibed without paying attention to the ancient scripture of *Bhagvad Gita* which is highly revered and adhered to. In course of his conversation, Lord Krishna explains that, "by developing purity of intention, passions directed towards mundane objects die producing tranquility of mind which in turn gives rise to the inward silence in which the soul begins to establish contact with the Eternal from which it is surrendered, and experience the presence of the Indwelling God" (*Radhakrishnan*, 2006). The emphasis is on emancipation and assimilation with the Almighty through renunciation. Any form of predilection towards mundane objects is thought of as an obstacle in the path to the God. The reason for this absolute disdain towards fulfillment of desire has been conveyed in the following lines, "whatever pleasures are born of the contacts (with objects) are only sources of sorrow, they have a beginning and an end, O! son of Kunti (Arjuna), no wise man delights in them" (Radhakrishnan, 2006). Thus, the *Bhagvad Gita* advocates detachment from desires.

Further, the difficulty in attaining this end too has been widely acknowledged and means have been suggested. Lord Chaitanya, a highly revered 13th century Indian saint, believed that, "by chanting the holy name of the Lord one can directly associate with the Supreme Lord by sound vibration. As one practices this sound vibration, he passes through three stages of development: the offensive stage, the clearing stage and the transcendental stage. In the offensive stage one may desire all kinds of material happiness, but in the second stage one becomes clear of all material contaminations. When one is situated in the transcendental stage, he attains the most coveted position—the stage of loving God" (*Prabhupada,* 1995, p. x). It is a representative statement of a majority of schools of thought which believed in the inferiority of material happiness *vis-à-vis* the attainment of spiritual enlightenment. *AC* Bhaktivedanta Swami Prabhupada (1995, p. xi) further goes on to propagate that, "being engaged in the superior activities of Krsna consciousness, superior men naturally retire from the inferior activities of material existence."

However, the Indian culture is not without its share of critiques of this meta-physical perspective of materialism (*see http://www.wikipedia.org/materialism*). In ancient Indian philosophy, materialism developed around 600 BCE with the works of Ajita Kesakambali, Payasi and the proponents of *Charvaka* School of philosophy. Payasi, a 6th century BC materialist philosopher has written in *Payasi—sutanta*, as quoted by Chattopadhyaya (1993), "Neither is there any other world, nor are there beings reborn otherwise than from parents, nor is there fruit or result of deed well-done or ill-done." The words may sound iconoclastic but the tone of these early materialists seem to be one of rebellion against anti-materialism rather than conviction in materialism.

However, the *Charvaka* system of Indian philosophy, also known as *Lokayata*, was more brazen in its advocacy of materialism. This branch of Indian philosophy is not considered to be part of the six orthodox schools of Hinduism—*Nyaya* and *Vaisheshika. Mimansa* and *Vedanta, Samkhya* and *Yoga*—which recognise the authority of the *Vedas* as divine revelation and function as pairs (*Beck*, 2003). An important contributor to the *Charvaka* philosophy was Brihaspati who authored *Sarvadarsana Sangraha* wherein he enunciated the principle–

> *"Yavvajivet sukham jivet; Rinam kritvaa ghritam pibet; Bhasmibhutasya Dehasya; Punaraagamanam kutah."*

This is the seventh verse and may be translated as

> As long as you live, live happily; Take a loan and drink *ghee*;
>
> After a body is reduced to ashes; Where will it come back from?

The *Charvakas* adopted and disseminated the idea that good living, symbolised by *ghee,* was the route to self-fulfillment. Though, this philosophy of materialism was criticised, however scholars acknowledged its acceptance among the people as is evident from the following words written by Madhavacharya, a 14th century philosopher, in his work *Sarvadarsana Sangraha*, " The efforts of *Charvaka* are indeed hard to be eradicated, for the majority of living beings hold by the current refrain: While life is yours, live joyously; None can escape Death's searching eye; When once this frame of ours they burn; How shall it e'er again return?".

The existence and development of contradictory beliefs only contributed towards the significance of materialism in Indian culture. In this context, the present research assumes greater degree of importance as it intends to empirically examine materialism among Indians, which has theoretically existed and has been a subject of much dialectic for last 2,500 years.

Materialism—Insights for the Marketer

The text book definition of materialism states that it is a personality-like trait which distinguishes between individuals who regard possessions as essential to their identities and their lives and those for whom possessions are secondary (Schiffman and Kanuk, 2005, p. 157-158). Belk (1984, 1985) viewed materialism as an integration of personality traits—possessiveness, non-generosity and envy. Belk (1987) defined materialism as "the tendency to believe that consumer goods and services provide the greatest source of satisfaction and dissatisfaction in life." Richins and Dawson (1992) conceptualised materialism as a value whose influence goes beyond mere consumption arenas and is based on three dimensions or "orienting values"—acquisition centrality, acquisition as the pursuit of happiness and possession defined success. They defined materialism as "a value that guides peoples' choices and conduct in a variety of situations but not limited to consumption arenas."

A metaphorical expression to illustrate the relationship between marketing and materialism can be that they are like Siamese twins who are mutually dependent. O Shaughnessy and O Shaughnessy (2002) believe that the tendency towards materialism is an inherent constituent of human condition and it was widespread prosperity which fuelled the emergence of both marketing activity and consumerist behaviour simultaneously.

The evidence from Sociology shows that the desire to possess material things is present in most cultures (*Mukerji*, 1983) and it could be because such a desire is a basic human characteristic (*Rubin*, 1986). It raises a very important question as to how does one differentiate the "materialistic" from the "mundane". The available research indicates towards the following differentiating criteria:

1. A strong belief that possessions give pleasure which leads to seeking pleasure through possession rather than through other means such as personal relationships, experiences and achievements (See *Richins* and *Dawson*, 1992). For materialists, the pursuit of possessions becomes a religion and possessions become an object of worship (*Bredemeier* and *Toby*, 1960).
2. Purchase decisions are not solely dependent upon the utilisation value of the product or service. Chandon *et. al.* (2000) have suggested that there are two dimensions of consumer value—utilitarian and hedonic. The utilitarian perspective is based on the assumption that consumers are rational problem solvers (*Bettman,* 1979) whereas hedonic consumption designates those aspects of consumer behaviour that relate to the multi-sensory, fantasy and emotive aspects of one's experience with products (*Hirschman* and *Holbrook*, 1982). The present author believes that a materialistic consumer is more of a *'Homo Ludens'* (a man guided by his senses and wants) than a *'Homo Economicus'* (utility calculator). This statement stands substantiated by the findings of Richins (1994a) that socially visible products that signal social status or prestige are valued more and have greater importance for materialistic consumers than do less socially visible products since they express socially embedded meanings for the owners. The reason may be attributed to the fact that materialist consumers use socially sanctioned objects to either announce their status or arouse audience reaction (*Fournier* and *Richins*, 1991). However, precisely because of this intense desire for better possessions in product categories with higher potential for status signaling makes them less satisfied with their possessions (*Wang* and *Wallendorf*, 2006). The present author believes that this dissatisfaction sends

the materialistic into an endless quest and un-fulfilled longing for products with greater hedonic value, thus ending up as *'Alice in Wonderland'*.

It is these characteristics of a materialistic consumer which makes it such a soft target for the marketer that even during low consumer confidence; it would urge consumers to splurge.

Materialism—Good or Bad

Materialism is generally viewed as a negative characteristic linked to traits like possessiveness, envy and lack of generosity or as a tendency to like possessions and gain pleasure from ownership (*Belk* 1984, 1985; *Richins* and *Dawson*, 1992; *Browne* and *Kaldenberg* (1997). Mick (1996) categorised materialism as one of the "dark side" variable. The genesis of such an interpretation probably lies in the fact that historically, all major religions have condemned materialism for the fear that worldly goods will replace the Supreme Being as the focus of worship (*Belk*, 1983, 1985). Some of the religions even go to the extent of advocating renunciation of material possessions as key to salvation or *moksha*. However, the present author believes that a more balanced and pragmatic view needs to be adopted since, as suggested by Belk (1987), both—the extremes of self-denial as well as self-gratification—need to be condemned. Research in medical science has shown that extreme forms of material denial may be related to orexia-nervosa, bulimia, masochism and other self-destructive tendencies (*Belk*, 1984; *D'Arcy*, 1967; *Masson*, 1976). On the contrary, people who are highly materialistic tend to report greater levels of anxiety and physical symptomatology (*Kasser* and *Ahuvia*, 2002).

Hence, materialism has been criticised by some; materialism has been admired by others, however, it is hard to ignore materialism since it is here to stay. This perception is shared by Venkatesh (1994), who opined that materialism would continue to remain the most distinctive characteristic of present consumerist world, especially in the very fast developing Asian economies like India.

The present author believes that materialism can not be categorised as either good or bad because, without materialism society may appear more puritan but without the opportunity to get spoilt, there would be no merit in virtue. To ward off the impact of downturn, marketers are advised to focus themselves on providing the consumer more and more opportunities to get spoilt.

REFERENCES

1. Belk, R.W. (1983), "Worldly Possessions: Issues and Criticisms," in *Advances in Consumer Research*, Vol. 10, Bagozzi, R.P. and A.M. Tybout, Association for Consumer Research, p. 514-519.
2. Belk, R.W. (1984), "Three Scales to Measure Constructs Related to Materialism: Reliability, Validity, and Relationships to Measures of Happiness," in Kinnear, T. (Ed.), *Advances in Consumer Research*, Vol. 11, The Association for Consumer Research, p. 291-297.
3. Belk, R.W. (1985), "Materialism: Trait Aspects of Living in a Material World", *Journal of Consumer Research*, Vol. 12, December, p. 265-280.
4. Belk, R.W. (1987), "Material Values in the Comics: A Content Analysis of Comic Books Featuring Themes of Wealth," *Journal of Consumer Research*, Vol. 14, June, p. 26-42.
5. Bettman, J.R. (1979), *An Information Processing Theory of Consumer Choice*, Addison-Wesley, Reading, MA.
6. Bredemeier, H. C. and J. Toby (1960), *Social Problems in America: Costs and Casualties in an Acquisitive Society*, Wiley, New York.
7. Browne, B.A. and D.O. Kaldenberg (1997), "Conceptualising Self-Monitoring: Links to Materialism and Product Involvement", *Journal of Consumer Marketing*, Vol. 14, No. 1, p. 31-44.
8. *Business Standard* (2009), "Value Buying Pushes-up Pantaloon's April Sales," Bhubaneswar Edition, 14 May.
9. Chandon, P., B. Wansink, and G. Laurent, (2000), "A Benefit Congruency Framework of Sales Promotion Effectiveness", *Journal of Marketing*, Vol. 64, No. 4, p. 65-81.
10. Chatterjee, S. and D. Datta (1984), *An introduction to Indian Philosophy*, 8th Ed., University of Calcutta.

11. Chattopadhyaya, D. (1993), *Indian Philosophy,* 7th Ed., People's Publishing House, New Delhi.

12. D'Arcy, P. F. (1967), "Asceticism (Psychology of)," in *New Catholic Encyclopaedia,* Vol. 1. McGraw-Hill: New York, pp. 941-942.

13. Fournier, S. and M.L. Richins, (1991), "Some Theoretical and Popular Notions Concerning Materialism", *Journal of Social Behaviour and Personality,* Vol. 6, p. 403-414.

14. Hirschman, E.C. and M.B. Holbrook (1982), "Hedonic Consumption: Emerging Concepts, Methods and Propositions", *Journal of Marketing,* Vol. 46, No. 3, p. 92-101.

15. http://en.wikipedia.org/wiki/Charvaka

16. http://en.wikipedia.org/wiki/Materialism

17. Kasser, T. and A.C. Ahuvia (2002), "Materialistic Values and Well-being in Business Students", *European Journal of Social Psychology,* Vol. 32, p. 137-146.

18. Masson, J. M. (1976), "The Psychology of the Acetic," *Journal of Asian Studies,* 35 (August), p.611-625.

19. Mick, D.G. (1996), "Are Studies of Dark Side Variables Confounded by Socially Desirable Responding? The Case of Materialism," *Journal of Consumer Research,* Vol. 23, September, p. 106.

20. Mukerji, C. (1983), *From Graven Images: Patterns of Modern Materialism,* New York: Columbia University Press.

21. O' Neil, William J. (2004), "Business Leaders and Success," Tata McGraw Hill Publishing Company Limited, New Delhi.

22. O'Shaughnessy, J. and N.J. O'Shaughnessy, (2002), "Marketing, the Consumer Society and Hedonism", *European Journal of Marketing,* Vol. 36, No. 5/6, p. 524-547.

23. Prabhupada, A. C. Bhaktivedanta Swami (1995), *Teachings of Lord Chaitanya: The Golden Avatar,* The Bhaktivedanta Book Trust.

24. Radhakrishnan, S (2006), *The Bhagvadgita,* 24th Impression, Harper Collins Publishers.

25. Richins, M.L. (1994a), "Special Possessions and the Expression of Material Values", *Journal of Consumer Research,* Vol. 21, p. 522-533.

26. Richins, M.L. and S. Dawson (1992), "A Consumer Values Orientation for Materialism and its Measurement: Scale

Development and Validation", *Journal of Consumer Research*, Vol. 19, p. 303-16.

27. Rubin, N. (1986), "It is the Season to be Greedy," *Parents*, 61 (December), p. 134-137, 217, 222-226.
28. Schiffman, L.G. and L.L. Kanuk (2005), *Consumer Behaviour*, 8th ed., PHI.
29. Venkatesh, A. (1994), "India's Changing Consumer Economy: A Cultural Perspective," Ad*vances in Consumer Research* Volume 21, p. 323-328.
30. Wang, J. and M. Wallendorf (2006), "Materialism, Status Signaling, and Product Satisfaction," *Journal of the Academy of Marketing Science*, Vol. 34, No. 4, p. 494-505.

CHAPTER **4**

Meaningful Management of All Assets of Public Sector Banks in India

—DR. SHIRISH R. KULKARNI
—CHIRAG P. SURTI

Since, introduction of economic reforms and implementation of prudential norms (as recommended by Shri *M. Narasimham Committee*) in early 90's, the adherence and meaningful compliance took some time in the Public Sector Banks. It was at this stage that some uniform practices emerged in assessing non-performing assets in Public Sector Banks. Good and effective regulatory system under stewardship of RBI and mandatory compliance to statutory audit as well as in house audit system backed by time bound stipulation triggered a lot of transparency in judging assets qualities of Public Sector Banks. It was then for the first time that income recognition, provisioning in respect of assets classification and stricter follow up for servicing interest cost, threw open more meaningful picture of balance sheet in Public Sector Banks. It was such a laborious exercise which helped management of Public Sector Banks to truly make judgement on their financial strength and weaknesses, besides taking a close look at threats and challenges. Management prudence, regulatory controls and mandatory compliance to prudential norms, net net resulted in first identifying existing NPA's, potential NPA's , adequate provisioning, strategically planned follow-up for upgradation and restructuring of NPA's, efficient fund management, augmenting of capital, retaining profits, carrying it forward in the balance sheet, periodical review of of assets liability mismatch etc. were focussed parameters under controlled reins of management which made balance sheet of Public Sector Banks more transparent, more analytical as well as more informative for taking bet or financial call on standing out each Public Sector Banks.

Status of Public Sector Banks balance sheet as stated in above referred para, together with time bound compliance to Basel I as also sufficient initiatives and actions taken for compliance to Basel II norms, have given lot of comfort and competence to management of Public Sector Banks, not only in achieving meaningful reduction of NPA's between 2000 to 2006 but also threw opportunities to plan and manage credit profile in such a way that Public Sector Banks could arrest slippages in respect of potential NPA's in time and discover working remedies to address sickness well in advance. Even historically weak banks which were flooded with age old NPA's and with substantial inadequacy of capital like Dena Bank, UCO Bank, Indian Bank etc. also could find fever from Government of India for infusing fresh capital through budgetory support and not only they survive but these weak banks finally joined elite club of those Public Sector Banks which have achieved mandatory stipulated NPA's ratio of less than 3 per cent and capital adequacy ratio of more than 9 per cent. This speaks volumes of prudence shown and demonstrated by PSB's in India against collapsing finanacial sector in world economy more particularly economies in U.S and Europe. Needless to mentioned that over 100 banks went bankrupt during crisis of 2008 onwards till date that financial system in India—both in Private and Public Sector Banks stood rock like firm with substantial strength not only to stage first singn of recovery from the recession in the world but also presented and registered mind boggling IIP (Indian Industrial Production) numbers as also show casing high catching growth and revival in service sector together with reversal of a trend in agriculture sector and exports in our country.

While full credit goes to timely actions taken by Central Bank (RBI) on monetory stance and credit policy reviewed from time to time and able support from ministry of finance in exercising fiscal prudence, India has emerged as strongest economic power and most favoured destination in the globe. In a situation like this very ambitious Indian entrepreneur and Indian corporate, understandably remain aggressively inspired for growth and expansion to tape potential of stupendous economic growth pegged at 8 per cent to 9 per cent in the coming couple of financial years as also Government of India with a clear political mandate remaining in power for next three years, throws open huge opporunities for capital incentive expenditure. We are a country over 100 billion population and 70 per cent of such population being less than 35 in age, represent youngest country in the world. Obviously young average age group strong potential economic growth aimed at double digit growth, very sound fundamental vibrant but significantly regulated stock market with robust system in place, very sensible chemistry emerging between Central Bank (RBI) and ministry of finance, are clearly supporting prospects of India emerging as super economic power and player in the world economy and such a condition will accelerated pace transforming status of developing economy into developed economy. Needless to mentioned here that this will ensure substantial improvement in the standard of living of all classes which will give major triggered to consumption pattern in the country which can lead to inflationary pressures while country's Central Bank and Government both have been fighting restlessly against raising prices in food articles and improve supply side of constrainst, the challenges have not cased as yet.

It is in time like this that relook at prudential norms in management of NPA's with more innovative, dynamic and aggressive outlook would help manage situation like mortgage prices of U.S. or sovereign credit defaults as recently experienced in Greece, Portugal, Spain and other Eurozone country. We at India, are nicely placed to take a look at U.S.

recessionary triggered of yesterday and sovereign credit default in Eurozone today. While it is not wise to think that we are decoupled with either forces, it is definitely of opportunity to set in motion, strong , strong under current to tackle eventual situation should it happen in our country either during transition phase from developing economy to developed economy or should such things happen after our country assumes the status of developed economy. In short it is today time has matured to walk an extra mile in advance for preparing ourselves to mitigate economic blues, should they occur. Therfore substantial qualitatives and quantitatives improvement in efficient and meaningful management of all assets (and not only NPA's) is necessary. Undersign is therefore of views that a committee comprises of experts should be formed with recommendation of Central Bank and Ministry of Finance. Proper presentation should be given in formation of committee to India Inc heads of PSB's , Private Banks and Foreign Banks reputed economists, farmers and representatives of cottage industries, educationalist or top ranked faculties of best business schools of the country. Such a committee should be asked to submit their reports and recommendation to finance commissioner of the country within a six month time which should broadly outline revised norms for management and improvement of all the assets and not only NPA's.

Authors are of the opinion that maximum coverage should be given to under mentioned point in evolving revised prudential norms for management of all assets.

(1) Time has matured that money raised by PSB's, either in form of capital or by way of raising deposits from public and institutions or by borrowing money from other sources, should be closely tracked when so raised money is finding its way for utilisation either in form of cash and Bank balance or investment and lending or creation of fixed or any other type of assets. In short utilisation of money must be in line with purpose for which it is raised and so utilised money must performed in terms of economic viablity. Here authors

are lying emphasis on continous process of assessing performance of deployed money in form of *all types of assets, and not only take a myopia view to assess performance of only that money which is deployed by way of credit that is loans and advances.*

(2) For meaningful compliance to what is stated in point No. 1 above, PSB's are expected to take various steps including procedural changes, different types of book keeping, transparent system in which clear cut accountablity can be fixed. Firstly the authors suggest following changes to be made in the existing norms for management of NPA's in respect of Banks loans and advances.

(*a*) Bank must evolve a system established that funds realised by way of loans and advances is utilised for the purpose creating assets stated in the sanctioned proposal and the same have been verified by Banks resposible officials immediately on creation of such assets. Not only assets verification certificate/report should be placed on record by the verifying resposible official of the Bank but also the report should contain comprehensive discription of the assets including its make, its name of the suppliers, quality of the assets and very importantly the report should clearly state the age of assets on the date of verification and remaining economic life of the assets in the opinion of verifying officials. The report should also state clearly what are the basis to judge existing age of the assets and potential economic life left in the assets. This is very significant and important as the performance of the assets will totally depend on the relevant aspects and therefore Bank must provide sufficient technical and other allied support to inspecting officials for being judicious in his comment on these vital points.

(*b*) Above referred assets verification report will established enduse of funds has also the age of assets and economic life of assets will help Bank in deciding the course of action to be taken or monitoring performance of this assets vis a vis conduct of borrower account and financial transaction in the account.

(*c*) Irrespective of good or bad conduct of the borrower account, whether or not such account remains performing or non performing, Bank must evolve a table of year wise provision to be made on such account. Keeping purely in view the economic life of the assets financed. Needless to mentioned that judgement on economic life of the assets is very critical and pivotal point and should commensurate with repayment schedule. In simple words, the Bank should start making provision on loans and advances from day one in such a way that fully disbursed loan amount stands provided in that many number of years as are judge to be having economic life of the assets. This is to say that every year loan account must be provided for on pro rata basis for its loss of economic life, irrespective of fact whether conduct in the borrower account is satisfactory or not. In fact existing prudential norm have stipulated 0.25 per cent of provision even on standard assets and authors are only supplementing here to extend provision exercise on all standard assets year over year at regular intervals till assets out live its economic life.

(*d*) Exercise as above will translate into a drain over Banks profitablity on yearly basis. However such an exercise may have only temporary blip as in all cases of performing standard assets, the provision amount would be written back to profit and loss account at the end of repayment schedule and should account turn NPA at any given time during repayment time , then Bank may have ready source of provided funds from day one to cover the potential NPA's. such an exercise will not only strengthen Bank capacity to meet with contingent demands for covering bad debts but also such accounting norms may help Bank claim higher rating from rating agencies. In the opinion of author this is good time to ushering such a procedure because almost all PSB's have been successful in achieving 1 per cent or more on return on assets besides very attractive ROE status, as also gross and net NPA's remaining respectively at less than 4 per cent and 2 per cent in all PSB's.

(3) With improved profitablity and well controlled NPA's, there has been an intangible attitude on part of PSB's management to adopt write off exercise in account of Rs. 100000 and less outstanding balance. Such an attitude and strategy was reasonable at a time , say in late 90's or early 2000 when Banks have triggered balancesheet cleaning-up of exercise. At that time Banks also wanted to off load the extra flab of that part of credit portfolio which represented politically motivated aggression by way of *loan mela* etc in pursuit of its socio-economic stature besides its very existance as Government owned organisation. Nevertheless, in todays contact Bank must endeavours to recover every rupee finance and the cost incurred on such finance, even if the account is well treated as loss asets with 100 per cent provisioning in place. Whether Rs. 100000 or less or even Rs. 25000 or less the Banks capacity to provide for NPA's adequately due to fate profits generated by them does not in any way entitle them to just write off 100% provided account and not recover dues there to persons resposible for status of NPA's must not got away whether they are borrowers on one side or Banks responsible officials on other side. Net amount if any that is written off must be recorded in the Banks book as judicious write off only on approval competent committee of the senior officers of the Bank

As regards assets other than loans and advances, the Bank must evolve a systematic procedure to make judgement on the performance of money deployed by the Bank and wherever performance of deployed money is not attaining the benchmark levels then Bank must take appropriate action to provide for non performance of other assets.

Few illustrative examples are given hereunder:

(*i*) All the borrowed funds should be so deployed remuneratively so that the cost of funds and service cost for such deployments of funds is fully recovered from the utilisation of such borrowed funds and not only that but even a reasonable margin should remain available to Bank. In simple words if deployments of borrowed fund do not service its entire cost then shortfall together with repayment instalment must be provided and such provision should be critically carried out in statutory audit every year.

(*ii*) After compliance of all statutory requirements the surplus funds must find. Such investments whose rate of return should out perform similar investment make by other financial organisation. This should be however a comparable exercise to monitor profits of the Banks and no provision would be necessary unless principal amount of investment get eroded on market to market basis.

(*iii*) Banks intangible assets such as over due outstanding balances in suspense account and claims made against the Banks or Banks claim on other remaining in dispute should be provided 100 per cent.

(*iv*) Banks investment in fixed assets must be critically assessed in terms of utilisation of such assets and its corresponding value to determine fair cost absorb by the Bank for investment made in such fixed assets. Illustratively if Bank has acquired a premises of 5000 sq ft involving total cost of Rs.50 lacs and if that premises after being ready for use, is either not utilise or under utilise then the difference between the cost of funds invested in the premises and income that would have been generated from utilisation of such premises, the difference there to should be provided.

Such an exercise will compel Bank management to take a prudent care either in liquidating the non remunerative fixed assets or profitablity utilised fixed assets for more income generation.

Conclusion

All above stated proposition can make financial organisation like Banks more stable, more transparent and more dependably reliable for its customers besides creating substantial strength in the country's economy.

REFERENCES

1. *The Reserve Bank of India Bulletin,* Published by Department of Econonic and Analysis and Policy, RBI, Mumbai.
2. *RBI Reports on Currency and Finance.* Various Issues, Mumbai.
3. *Book of Instruction,* Bank of Baroda.
4. Bank of India, Mumbai, *Head Office Circulars.*
5. *Indian Banking Association Bulletin,* Mumbai.
6. Modern Banking, Indian Institute of Banking and Finance, Mumbai.
7. *Banking Theory, Law and Practice* By Gordan, Natrajan, Himalaya Publishing House, Nagpur.
8. *Basics of Banking and Finance* By Dr. K.M. Bhattacharya , O.P. Agarwal Himalaya Publishing House, Bangalore.
9. *Financial Institutions and Markets, Structure, Growth and Innovations* By Dr. L. M. Bhole, Tata McGraw Hill Publishing Company Ltd, New Delhi.
10. *Economic and Political Weekly* (EPW), Mumbai

CHAPTER 5

Introduction and Overview of E-Commerce and M-Commerce

—RAJESH D. SHELKE

ABSTRACT

Electronic commerce is more than selling stuff online; it's using online resources and tools to do business better more efficiently and productively. It's about making and saving money online. The term e-commerce is used because transaction takes place using electronic communication and not paper communication. These transactions includes orders sent to vendors to supply items, invoices sent by vendors, payments made using electronic funds transfer and cash payments made using what is known as e-cash. The important points to note are that all transactions are carried out electronically using the Internet. There are commonly known as Business to Business (B2B), Business to Consumer (B2C) and Customer to Customer (C2C) e-commerce. E-commerce can work for any business because it involves the whole business cycle from production, procurement, distribution, sales, payment, fulfillment, restocking, and marketing. It's about relationships with customers, employees, suppliers, and distributors. It involves support services like banks, lawyers, accountants, and government agencies. Mobile commerce or m-commerce is a subject of e-commerce that deals with electronic transactions using mobile communication equipments. M-commerce is done in a wireless environment, via the Internet, private communication lines or other infrastructure. M-commerce is not merely a variation on existing Internet services: it is a natural extension of e-business. M-commerce involves exchanging Internet contents with a network of mobile people via wireless devices. Many of the e-commerce applications are done in m-commerce .For example, m-banking, m-shopping, m-music and the like.

Keywords

E-commerce, E-cash, M-commerce, Procurement

Introduction to Electronic Commerce(E-Commerce)

The internet has brought about a dramatic change in the ways business is done in today's world. It is seen that one of the important issues being faced by organisations around the world is how to build an effective e-business strategy and the relevant technology choices involved thereof. It is pertinent to note in this context that it is not technology alone but how one uses the technology to transform the business processes. In fact, one of the key parameters in which companies are being evaluated for their marketing efficiency is how well they can adopt themselves to the internet and exploits the advantage of the e-business.

The first step understands what exactly are the opportunities and challenges presented by the advent of e-business to the business. Every company must learn to implement far reaching changes within it to take advantage of the new ways the internet allows to perform such functions as purchasing, customer service, marketing and distribution and interaction with business partners. The more an organisation can use the internet to tie together the corporate infrastructure goals and technology, the more effective it will be in realising its goals and success.

Although much of this course focuses on using the World Wide Web, it is important to state at the outset electronic commerce is more than web-based commerce. It involves all types of communications technology, including the WWW, email, private bulletin board systems or value-added networks, intranets and extranets. It uses all forms of communications technology: email, testing, television, fax, mobile and landline phones.

Electronic commerce is more than selling stuff online; it's using online resources and tools to do business better more efficiently and productively. It's about making and saving money online.

E-commerce can work for any business because it involves the whole business cycle from production, procurement, distribution, sales, payment, fulfillment, restocking, and marketing. It's about relationships with customers, employees, suppliers, and distributors. It involves support services like banks, lawyers, accountants, and government agencies.

According to the Census Bureau: "E-commerce (or electronic commerce) is any business transaction whose price or essential terms were negotiated over an online system such as an Internet, Extranet, Electronic Data Interchange network, or electronic mail system."

Ever since the advent of the Internet, the World Wide Web and ISPs a revolution has taken place in the way business is carried out. This world wide telecommunication infrastructure has initiated a number of innovations in business conducted between business organisation between individual and business and between individuals and individuals. There are commonly known as Business to Business (B2B), Business to Consumer (B2C) and Customer to Customer (C2C) e-commerce. The term e-commerce is used because transaction takes place using electronic communication and not paper communication. These transactions includes orders sent to vendors to supply items, invoices sent by vendors, payments made using electronic funds transfer and cash payments made using what is known as e-cash. The important points to note are that all transactions are carried out electronically using the Internet. We may define e-commerce as "the sharing of business information, maintaining business, relationships and conducting business transactions using telecommunications networks. There are a variety of e-commerce applications including the following :

1. Retail stores such as book stores, music stores known as e-shops.
2. Banks connected to their customers providing services such as deposits, payments, giving account status etc.
3. Railways/airlines, cinema tickets, booking on-line form home and paying for it by credit cards or on delivery.
4. Advertising on the World Wide Web through certain free services.

The above applications are between business such as stores, banks, railways etc. and customers and are classified as (B2C) e-commerce.

The following are classified as Government to customer (G2C) e-commerce.

1. Filling tax returns with government agencies on-line and obtaining an immediate acknowledgement.
2. Getting government rules/regulations forms etc. from Internet kiosks.

Business to Business (B2B) e-commerce application include

1. Business ordering supplies from vendors using the Internet or a private network.
2. Banks carrying out transactions among themselves using a private network.
3. Business publishing catalogues on their website, thereby saving money in printing and distribution.

Customer to Customer (C2C) e-commerce Applications Include

1. Individual advertising items for sale using an intermediary's website address.
2. Auction sites using which an individual buyer or seller can buy or sell goods.
3. Electronic publishing of scholar/articles/stories by individual.

Stages in e-business Cycle

There are four different stages in the e-business cycle which are given below :

1. Transforming core business procedures.
2. Building flexible, expandable e-business applications.
3. Creating a scalable, available, safe environment and finally.
4. Leveraging the knowledge and information gained through the e-business and the best practices, which can be replicated.

Benefits of e-business to an Organisation

The following are some of the important benefits, which could accrue for an organisation due to the deployment of e-business initiatives.

1. Improved customer service
2. Improved customer retention rates
3. Slash operating costs
4. Enhance product/service quality
5. Improve business efficiency
6. Improve competitiveness
7. Improve business intelligence
8. Extended market coverage
9. Slash administrative errors

Advantages and Disadvantages of e-commerce

The major advantage to a customer using this mode of shopping is

1. One can buy /sell items from anywhere using one's computer provided an internet connection is available.
2. The shopping can be done 24 hours a day 365 days in a year.
3. One can avail of services such as financial services, legal services, medical advice, railway reservation etc. from appropriate portals.
4. Wider variety of goods are accessible easily without our spending time and money in physically visiting and searching in many shops.
5. Anonymous friendly advice may be available on items one may like to buy/rent.

The advantage which accrue to a business are

1. With a website a business can reach out to a world wide customer base at a very low cost.
2. Order processing cost is reduced as manual data entry is reduced. Business is also carried out faster as all documents are exchanged electronically.
3. Inventory size is reduced as transaction time is reduced.
4. Funds transfer is faster.
5. A large number of potential business partners can be quickly found and contacted using appropriate search engines and e-mail correspondence.
6. In some cases middlemen such as retailers can be eliminated as a manufacturer or assemblers of customized goods can reach out directly to a customer, this reaches out cost and delays.

The Major Disadvantage of e-commerce is

1. Currently Internet access is not widely available in India specially in rural sector.

2. Communication infrastructure is expensive and not very reliable particularly to individuals in rural India.
3. Payment by credit cards requires faith in the system security .As of now there is no mutual trust between seller and buyer on this of payment using credit cards for goods and services ordered via Internet in India.
4. Electronic data interchange standards have to be in place before business to business e-commerce can increase. Small business may find it difficult to conform to these standards.
5. Many persons go shopping for social contacts, window shopping, touch and feel before buying items. E-commerce will de-personalise transactions.
6. A major concern is security of transactions on the Internet. Spies or hackers can steal and misuse credit cards number if appropriate care is not taken.
7. Portals have to protect by special security systems from virus attacks and other electronic problems.

In spite of this disadvantage e-commerce is bound to rapidly increase due to its convenience. Some of the security and privacy issues are not severe in business to business e-commerce using private networks connecting them.

Payments Scheme in e-commerce

Payments are an important component in e-commerce. In day to day commercial dealings, there are many modes of payment each with its own advantages and disadvantages. The most common payment especially for low value purchases, is by cash. For higher value purchases, credit cards are preferred by customers. If a customer is a trusted party, merchants normally accept cheque, payment for services such as telephone, electricity bills and settlement of bills between businesses is normally done by cheque. In e-commerce also we need systems which are equivalent to these three modes of payment. Of these three modes cash transaction is the one which is the most difficult to mimic. Large electronic cash transactions are discouraged by most governments.

Emerging Mobile Commerce

Mobile commerce or m-commerce is a subject of e-commerce that deals with electronic transactions using mobile communication equipments. M-commerce is done in a wireless environment, via the Internet, private communication lines or other infrastructure. There are two major characteristics of m-commerce that differentiate it from other forms of e-commerce. They are mobility and broad reach. M-commerce is based on the fact that users carry a cell phone or other mobile device everywhere they go. Mobility implies portability. Moreover with m-commerce people can be reached at any time, anywhere.

M-commerce is not merely a variation on existing Internet services: it is a natural extension of e-business. M-commerce involves exchanging Internet contents with a network of mobile people via wireless devices. Many of the e-commerce applications are done in m-commerce. For example, m-banking, m-shopping, m-music and the like.

M-commerce is done with the help of mobile communication equipments and they include 'Smart phones' and 'Personal digital assistants'. Smart phones are internet–enabled cell phones that can support mobile applications. These 'phones with a brain' are becoming standard devices. Personal digital assistant (PDA) is a small portable computer, such as the family of palm handhelds and the pocket PC devices. Wireless Application Protocol (WAP) is the technology that offers internet browsing from wireless devices. Global Positioning system (GPS) is a satellite-based tracking system that enables determination of a devices location.

The messages sent through these mobile communication equipments may be in the form of SMS, EMS or MMS. Short Message Service (SMS) is a technology in existence since

1991 that allows for the sending short text messages on certain cell phones. Data are borne by the radio resources reserved in cellular networks for locating mobile devices and connecting calls. SMS messages can be sent or received concurrently, even during a voice or data calls. Used by hundreds of million of users, SMS is known as the e-mail of m-commerce. Enhance messaging service (EMS) is an extension of SMS that is capable of simple animation, tiny pictures and short melodies. Multimedia messaging service (MMS) is the next generation of wireless messaging which delivers rich media.

M-commerce in India

M-commerce market in India has not seen as much growth as was expected. Experts opine that it is still in a very nascent stage and will take time to reach the maturity level to match European and US standards. Indian cellular operators are under tremendous pressure to sustain and grow their average revenue per user. Fierce competition among operators has consistently driven down tariffs, reducing revenue from the voice based operations of the wireless networks. So operators are providing value added services to sustain and grow.

If statistics are anything to go by, the SMS raga will drive m-commerce in India. The mobile industry is quite optimistic about the future of m-commerce. Wireless is considered to be the next big thing in the communications industry. The growth rate of mobile phones has already outnumbered the growth of fixed line phones in India. Once a secure easy-to-use method for paying over a mobile is devised, m-commerce will become a reality.

Information Technology Act 2000

1. This act provides the legal infrastructure for e-commerce in India. The object of the act has been stated as
2. E-mail correspondence has legal status and therefore it can be used in evidence. Digitally signed documents are now recognised

3. All applications to government bodies can be filled in electronic form .Government can issue licences, permits, sanctions, approaches on line in electronic form
4. The IT act provides statutory remedy to companies whose networks are illegally accessed and stored data is stolen.

The Top 10 Myths about e-commerce

1. Building an e-commerce site enables businesses to trade with no complications
2. The moment a businesses can accept credit cards and Pay Pal, it becomes global
3. E-commerce will boost the finances of any business
4. Customers will stumble on a company's site easily; there is no need to do additional marketing or merchandising.
5. Businesses cannot market products aggressively online if they sell their products through a reseller.
6. E-commerce is a project for the IT department and requires little outside input
7. Aggressive marketing will create bad will with customers
8. Ease of site navigation is not a major factor
9. Potential customers will assume that a company's site is legitimate
10. Companies cannot sell directly to the SMB market via websites

REFERENCES

1. Chaudhury, Abijit; Jean-Pierre Kuilboer (2002). *e- Business and e-Commerce Infrastructure*. McGraw-Hill.
2. Frieden, Jonathan D.; Roche, Sean Patrick (2006-12-19), "E-Commerce: Legal Issues of the Online Retailer in Virginia" (PDF), *Richmond Journal of Law and Technology* 13 (2).

3. Graham, Mark (2008), "Warped Geographies of Development: The Internet and Theories of Economic Development" (PDF), *Geography Compass* 2 (3): 771.
4. Kessler, M. (2003). More Shoppers Proceed to Checkout Online. Retrieved January 13, 2004.
5. Nissanoff, Daniel (2006). *Future Shop: How the New Auction Culture Will Revolutionise the Way We Buy, Sell and Get the Things We Really Want* (Hardcover ed.). The Penguin Press, p. 246.
6. Seybold, Pat (2001). *Customers.com.* Crown Business Books (Random House).
7. Miller, Roger (2002). *The Legal and E-Commerce Environment Today* (Hardcover ed.). Thomson Learning, p. 741.
8. Beynon-Davies P. (2004). E-Business. Palgrave, Basingstoke.
9. Paul Timmers, (2000), Electronic Commerce—Strategies and Models for Business-to-business Trading, p. 31, John Wiley and Sons, Ltd.

CHAPTER 6

Internet Banking in India—*Future Outlook*

—DR. R.K. UPPAL
—POONAM RANI

ABSTRACT

In the present day banking, total automation of banking operations is an imperative need for all banks to attract more customers, provide efficient services, and survive in the emerging new competition, apart from the profit motive which is the primary objective of the business. In order to achieve these goals of business, various channels have been developed through technology. 'Internet Banking' is one of the best alternative channels available to customers for quick, correct and efficient service at anytime and anywhere. The present paper is devoted to explore the extent of Internet banking in Indian banking industry. Time period taken for study is 2000-01 to 2006-07 because this period is the eye-witness of infant condition of IT and during the same period IT became mature. Simple statistical tools like average, standard deviation, co-efficient of variation are used to calculate the efficiency of various bank groups providing the service of I-banking. On the basis of analysis, the paper concludes that the private sector banks are on the top in providing the I-banking services to their customers and have high profitability as compared to other bank groups under study except foreign banks. The paper also highlights the benefits of I-banking to customers as well as to bankers and suggests some strategies with their possible solutions like to spread awareness regarding I-banking and to increase its area and scope to enhance I-banking services in India, particularly in rural and semi-urban areas.

Keywords

Extent of Internet Banking, Strategies to Enhance I-banking Services.

Introduction

Competition and the constant changes in technology and lifestyles have changed the face of banking. Now-a-days, banks are seeking alternative ways to provide and differentiate amongst their varied services. Customers, both corporate as well as retail, are no longer willing to queue in banks, or wait on the phone, for the most basic of services. They demand and expect to be able to transact their financial dealings where and when they wish to. With the number of computers increasing every year, the electronic delivery of banking services is becoming the ideal way for banks to meet their clients' expectations. The use of information technology in banking is now inherent in banking industry. A customer can log on banks website and access his account. He can perform following functions online: Balance enquiry, Transfer of funds and online payment. Internet banking refers to the use of Internet as a remote delivery channel for banking services. Web based or internet banking is poised to become the future face of banking services. The number of visits to the bank can be minimised effectively by operating from the Internet account. Thus the number of contacts required to perform a transaction and solve a problem has been reduced through online banking. The usual branches of banks have culminated into PC networks, whereby the consumer can draw all the benefits and services of the bank at a single click of the mouse. Internet banking can be categorised in following stages:

- ***Information Kiosks:*** Traditional information on banking products and services are available on the website of the bank.
- ***Basic I-Banking:*** Here, bank sets up infrastructure for Internet banking and for accessing basic services like opening an account, paying utility bills and checking the balance.
- ***Virtual Medium:*** Here Internet is taken as an official medium for financial transactions. Buying and selling activities can be undertaken through banks payment gateway technology. Today most of the banks are having their own functional websites through which banks are serving customers. There are more than 90 banks offering internet banking. Internet banking is now being accepted.

Development of Internet Banking in India

The financial reforms that were initiated in the early 1990s and the globalisation and liberalisation measures brought in a completely new operating environment to the banks. The bankers are now offering innovative and attractive technology-based services and products such as 'Anywhere Anytime Banking', 'Tele-Banking', 'Internet Banking', 'Web Banking', etc. to their customers to cope with the competition. The process started in the early 1980s when Reserve Bank of India (RBI) set up two committees in quick succession to accelerate the pace of automation of operations in the banking sector. A high-level committee was formed under the chairmanship of Dr. C. Rangarajan, then Governor of RBI, to draw up a phased plan for computerisation and mechanisation in the banking industry over a five-year time frame of 1985–1989. The focus by this time was on customer service and two models of branch automation were developed and implemented. Having gained experience in the earlier mode of computerisation, the second Rangarajan committee constituted in 1988 drew up a detailed perspective plan for computerisation of banks and for extension of automation to other areas such as funds transfer, e-mail, BANKNET, SWIFT, ATMs, i-banking, etc. The Government of India enacted the Information Technology Act, 2000 (generally known as IT Act, 2000), with effect from 17 October 2000 to provide legal recognition to electronic transactions and other means of electronic commerce. RBI had set up a 'Working Group' on i-banking to examine different aspects of i-banking. The Group had focussed on three major areas of i-banking such as (1) technology and security issues; (2) legal issues; and (3) regulatory and supervisory issues. RBI had accepted the recommendations of the 'Working Group', and accordingly issued guidelines on 'Internet banking in India' for implementation by banks. The 'Working Group' has also issued a report on i-banking covering different aspects of i-banking. Internet banking in India is currently at a nascent stage. While there are scores of companies specialising in developing i-banking software, security software and website designing and maintenance, there are few online financial service providers. ICICI bank is the first one to have introduced i-banking for a limited range of services such as access to account information, correspondence and, recently, funds transfer between its branches. ICICI is also getting into e-trading, thus offering a broader range of integrated services to the customer.

BENEFITS OF INTERNET BANKING TO CUSTOMERS AND TO BANKS

Benefits to Customers

- Convenience
- Tailored products and services
- Ease of access
- Ease of changing supplier

- Low cost
- Financial planning capability
- Consumers can use their computers and a telephone modem to dial in from home or any site where they have access to a computer
- The services are available seven days a week, 24 hrs a day

Benefits to Banks

- Cost saving
- Reaching new segment of the population
- Bring efficiency
- Enhancement of bank's reputation
- Better customer service
- Increase customer loyalty
- Attract new customers
- 24×7 client-servicing- for general services

II
REVIEW OF LITERATURE

Avasthi and Sharma (2000-01) have analysed in their study that advances in technology are set to change the face of banking business. Technology has transformed the delivery channels by banks in retail banking. It has also impacted the markets of banks. The study also explored the challenges that banking industry and its regulator face.

B. Janki (2002) analysed that how technology is affecting the employees' productivity. There is no doubt, in India particularly public sector banks will need to use technology to improve operating efficiency and customer services. The focus on technology will increase like never before to add value to customer services, develop new products, strengthen risk management etc. the study concludes that technology is the only tool to achieve their goals.

Bhasin (2001) analysed the impact of IT on banking sector. It has transformed the repetitive and overlapping systems and procedures into simple single key pressing technology resulting in speed, accuracy and efficiency of conducting business and enabling them to enter into the new activities.

De Young (2001). Indeed the use of the Internet as a new alternative channel for the distribution of financial services has become a competitive necessity instead of just a way to achieve competitive advantage with the advent of globalisation and fiercer competition.

Karjaluoto et al. (2002) Internet banking offer services regardless of geography and time and banks thus provide its services to the customers for them to use at their convenience.

Pikkarainen, Pikkarainen, Karjaluoto, and Pahnila, (2004) defines Internet banking as an 'Internet portal, through which customers can use different kinds of banking services ranging from bill payment to making investments'. With the exception of cash withdrawals, Internet banking gives customers access to almost any type of banking transaction at the click of a mouse.

Robinson (2000) believes that the supply of Internet banking services enables banks to establish and extend their relationship with the customers. There are other numerous advantages to banks offered by online banking such as mass customisation to suit the likes of each user, innovation of new products and services, more effective marketing and communication at lower costs.

Rao (2002) analysed the impact of new technology on banking sector. The technology is changing the way the business is done and opened new vistas for doing the same work differently in most cost effective manner. Tele-banking and Internet banking are making forays such that branch banking may give to home banking. He provided some policies to protect their profitability.

Shastri (2001) analysed the effect and challenges of new technology for banks. Technology has brought a sea change in the functioning of the banks. The earlier manual system of preparing of vouchers, etc. is slowing being automated thereby saving a lot of time and effort. The use of ATMs and introduction of more than in the past, especially in the Post-VRS Scenario.

Vageesh (2000) highly appreciated the new private sector banks which have adopted IT. The new private sector banks with their state-of-the-art technology and grandiose plans to make inroads into e-banking, are now darlings of the stock markets. Banks like HDFC and ICICI are foraying into net banking offering great convenience to customers on one hand and results in lower transaction cost for the banks on the other hand.

Research Gap

The review of studies clearly indicates that no comprehensive study has been undertaken regarding the extent of Internet banking among various e-channels and the extent of Internet banking using customers in India. Therefore, the present study is devoted to fulfill this gap and also to analyse the profit and business per employee of those bank groups providing more services through Internet banking.

III
OBJECTIVES, RESEARCH METHODOLOGY AND DATA BASE

Objectives

- To explore the extent of Internet banking among various e-channels.
- To know the extent of I banking using customers in various bank groups.
- To make strategies to enhance I-banking services in India.

Research Methodology

The research design of the paper is related to e-technology in Indian banking sector. The present paper focuses on I-banking services of various bank groups. The whole banking industry makes the universe of the study excluding RRB's and Co-operative banks. Indian banking industry has been divided into five groups as per the RBI guidelines.

G-I – SBI and Associate Banks (8)

G-II – Other Nationalised Banks (20)

G-III – Old Private Sector Banks (17)

G-IV – New Private Sector Banks (8)

G-V – Foreign Banks (29)

We have deliberately taken the period in the post IT Act of 2000 because after this period e-technology became mature in India. The study relates with the time period of 2000 to 2007. Some statistical tools like Mean, S.D, C.V, has been calculated to compare the various results and to get the desired results..

Data Base

- Report on Trend and Progress, RBI, 2006-07.
- IBA, Performance Highlights 2000-06.
- Information collected from the head offices of many banks.

IV
RESULTS AND DISCUSSION

To know the extent of I-banking in Indian banking industry, it is imperative to know the extent of branches of different bank groups providing the service of internet banking and the extent of customers availing this facility. Tables 6.1 to 6.5 show the extent of branches providing the facility of I-banking for different bank groups differently. These tables also show the position of I-banking among different e-channels.

Position of I-banking among various e-channels (G-I)

Table 6.1 shows the position of I-banking among different e-channels in G-I. It is clear that G-I has 95.55 pc computerized branches. After that comes the number of branches providing the facility of ATMs and Internet banking. Their average percentage is 35.43 and 30.04 respectively. G-I has only 30.04 per cent branches providing the facility of I-banking.

Table 6.1 (G-I) Position of I-banking among various e-channels

(Per cent)

E-Delivery Channel	2000-2001	2001-02	2002-03	2003-04	2004-05	2005-06	2006-07	Average
Computerized Branches	93.29	93.80	94.34	94.31	93.98	99.13	100	95.55
ATM	23.01	30.89	34.87	36.55	37.76	39.09	45.90	35.43
I-banking	11.80	16.25	23.08	32.27	35.08	40.37	51.44	30.04
M-banking	7.37	8.82	10.64	12.42	19.53	17.53	25.89	14.6
T-banking	3.69	4.41	6.68	9.50	12.30	13.62	19.38	9.94
Average	27.38	30.83	33.92	37.01	39.73	41.94	48.52	35.11

Source: Information Collected from Head Offices

Position of I-banking among Various e-channels (G-II)

In case of G-II, results are more depressing. It has only 4.35 per cent branches providing the service of internet banking. Although, Tele-banking have even less branches than I-banking but this statistics are not satisfactory for a country like India where population is availing the facility of Internet.

Table 6.2 (G-II) Position of I-banking among various e-channels

(Per cent)

E-Delivery Channel	2000-2001	2001-02	2002-03	2003-04	2004-05	2005-06	2006-07	Average
Computerised Branches	30.52	47.90	63.72	73.41	87.04	92.94	92.91	69.77
ATM	10.07	11.29	11.78	12.58	14.06	19.40	25.47	14.95
I-banking	1.55	1.94	2.74	4.21	5.01	6.65	8.40	4.35
M-banking	1.86	2.19	3.35	8.70	10.05	15.23	18.53	8.55
T-banking	0.94	1.37	2.96	3.53	3.86	6.10	11.40	4.30
Average	8.98	12.93	16.91	20.48	24.00	28.06	31.34	20.38

Source: Same as Table 6.1.

Position of I-banking among various e-channels (G-III)

In case of G-III also, position of Internet banking is not satisfactory. It has only 15.31 per cent Internet banking branches. Computerised and ATM branches are comparatively on better position.

Table 6.3 (G-III) Position of I-banking among various e-channels

E-Delivery Channel	2000-2001	2001-02	2002-03	2003-04	2004-05	2005-06	2006-07	Average
Computerised Branches	19.69	23.15	46.31	48.59	67.21	71.09	73.19	49.89
ATM	11.81	16.42	22.39	22.67	27.35	62.36	75.41	34.05
I-banking	6.25	7.98	15.05	15.60	17.68	20.71	23.93	15.31
M-banking	6.91	7.17	12.55	13.57	13.44	17.79	21.52	13.27
T-banking	5.74	8.83	10.90	11.44	13.31	18.47	20.64	12.76
Average	10.08	12.71	21.44	22.37	27.79	38.08	42.93	25.05

Source: Same as Table 6.1

Position of I-banking among various e-channels (G-IV)

In case of G-IV, the position of all e-channels is quite satisfactory. All branches of G-IV are fully computerised and G-IV has been observed the maximum average of internet banking as compared to other e-delivery channels.

Table 6.4 (G-IV) Position of I-banking among various e-channels

E-Delivery Channel	2000-2001	2001-02	2002-03	2003-04	2004-05	2005-06	2006-07	Average
Computerised Branches	100	100	100	100	100	100	100	100
ATM	40.66	42.51	58.58	51.65	81.84	89.03	83.60	63.98
I-banking	74.16	72.97	80.80	77.96	62.87	74.22	66.27	72.75
M-banking	64.59	69.63	72.72	71.21	56.59	69.26	61.04	66.43
T-banking	38.27	46.25	65.85	57.57	49.74	41.92	39.25	48.40
Average	63.53	66.27	75.59	71.67	70.20	74.88	70.03	70.31

Source: Same as Table 6.1

Position of I-banking among various e-channels (G-V)

Although, G-V has less number of I-banking branches than G-IV but the comparative position of it in G-V is better. It has 50.17 per cent branches providing the facility of Internet banking.

Table 6.5 (G-V) Position of I-banking among various e-channels

E-Delivery Channel	2000-2001	2001-02	2002-03	2003-04	2004-05	2005-06	2006-07	Average
Computerised Branches	100	100	100	100	100	100	100	100
ATM	132.85	130.61	217.22	188.94	294.32	169.63	202.42	190.85
I-banking	42.14	45.57	47.22	41.93	78.01	47.98	48.98	50.17
M-banking	40.71	40.13	45.00	44.23	75.88	46.96	50.20	49.01
T-banking	42.14	45.57	43.88	40.09	63.82	44.53	59.91	48.56
Average	71.56	72.37	90.66	83.03	122.40	81.69	92.30	87.71

Source: Same as Table 6.1

Comparative Position of Internet Banking among Various e-channels

Table 6.6 highlights the comparative position of Internet banking among different bank groups. It shows that G-IV is on the top position in providing the I-banking service to their customers. It has 73.75 per cent internet banking branches. G-V is on the second position and it has 50.17 per cent branches providing I-banking facility. Nationalised banks (G-II) has gained the last position to provide the Internet banking services *i.e.* only 4.35 per cent.

Table 6.6. Comparison of bank groups providing I-banking services

E-Delivery Channel	G-I	G-II	G-III	G-IV	G-V
Computerised Branches	95.55	69.77	49.89	100	100
ATM	35.43	14.95	34.05	63.98	190.85
I-banking	30.04	4.35	15.31	72.75	50.17
M-banking	14.6	8.55	13.27	66.43	49.01
T-banking	9.94	4.30	12.76	48.40	48.56
Overall Average	35.11	20.38	25.05	70.31	87.71

Source: Same as Table 6.1

Extent of Internet Banking using Customers

Table 6.7 shows the number of customers of different bank groups availing the service of internet banking in different years. It is clear from table that G-IV holds strong position among different bank groups. It has 5361893 customers in the year 2006-07 availing the facility of I-banking. In terms of number of customers using I-banking services, G-V and G-I gained second and third position respecItively. They have 2910125 and 2531141 internet banking users correspondingly. Compare to these three bank groups G-II and G-III have very less I-banking customers and they are 778599 and 189314 respectively. In all the bank groups customers of I-banking are increasing year by year this indicates the increasing popularity of I-banking.

Table 6.7 Customer using of Internet Banking Service

Bank Group	2000-01	2001-02	2002-03	2003-04	2004-05	2005-06	2006-07
G-I	25631	48963	84756	193141	576381	967544	2531141
G-II	12587	24632	43941	98849	158648	463191	778599
G-III	1880	9863	24963	42851	75911	97417	189314
G-IV	76509	121591	681494	998182	2244641	4656971	5361893
G-V	71625	99831	204117	504237	857677	1195601	2910125

Source: Same as Table 6.1

Net Profit as a Percentage of Working Funds

All the bank groups under study, more or less, are providing I-banking service to their customers. Among these bank groups, G-V and G-IV have maximum net profit as percentage of working funds. On an average, their net profit as percentage of working funds is 1.19 and 1.01 respectively. While G-III and G-I have gained next two positions. In case of G-II, net profit as percentage of working funds is only 0.79 per cent.

Table 6.8 Net profit as a percentage of working funds

(Per cent)

E-Delivery Channel	G-I	G-II	G-III	G-IV	G-V
2000-01	0.42	0.62	0.81	-0.72	0.71
2001-02	0.72	1.08	0.41	0.13	0.13
2002-03	0.96	1.17	0.90	1.57	1.56
2003-04	1.12	1.16	1.22	1.65	1.64
2004-05	0.89	0.22	1.13	1.30	1.29
2005-06	0.83	0.54	0.99	1.52	1.52
2006-07	0.85	0.76	0.92	1.65	1.47
Average	0.75	0.75	0.99	1.03	1.15
S.D.	0.22	0.31	0.30	0.76	0.46
C.V. (%)	29.33	41.33	30.30	73.78	40.00

Source: Performance Highlights, Various Issues, 2000 to 2007, IBA Mumbai

Business Per Employee of Various Bank Groups

Table 6.8 indicates the business per employee of different bank groups under study providing the service of Internet banking. The study reveals that foreign bank groups have maximum average of business per employee as compare to other bank groups. Foreign banks are more benefited than other bank groups. G-III and G-IV have almost same average of business per employee as shown in table. But on the other hand, public sector banks have very low average. Co-efficient of variation reveals that maximum variations found in G-I, G-II and G-V while least in G-III and G-IV.

Profit Per Employee of Various Bank Groups

Table 6.10 shows the profit per employee of those bank groups providing the facility of internet banking to their customers. It is clear from table that G-V (9.67 per cent) has maximum average of profit per employee followed by G-IV (7.42). In this respect, G-II gained the third & G-III gained the fourth position respectively. Their average of profit per employee is 2.48 and 1.77 per cent respectively. Co-efficient of variation reveals that the maximum variations found in G-II & G-V and comparatively less in other bank groups.

Table 6.9 Comparative Performance of Business per Employee in Various Bank Groups

(Per cent)

Years	G-I	G-II	G-III	G-IV	G-V
2000-01	1.60	2.00	7.46	9.03	159.93
2001-02	1.91	2.24	8.96	10.07	197.59
2002-03	2.15	2.99	10.94	10.31	221.90
2003-04	2.47	3.17	8.73	9.57	850.25
2004-05	3.06	3.55	8.75	9.40	307.62
2005-06	3.69	4.23	9.02	10.08	374.54
2006-07	4.61	4.96	8.11	9.95	434.05
Average	2.78	3.31	8.85	9.77	363.69
S.D.	1.07	1.05	1.07	0.45	235.99
C.V. (%)	34.48	31.72	12.09	4.60	64.88

Source: Same as Table 6.8.

Table 6.10 Comparative Performance of Profit per Employee in Various Bank Groups

(Per cent)

Years	G-I	G-II	G-III	G-IV	G-V
2000-01	0.77	0.41	0.94	5.12	-6.33
2001-02	1.21	1.03	1.83	3.88	1.23
2002-03	1.59	1.65	2.62	9.19	15.50
2003-04	2.00	7.65	2.76	9.59	15.29
2004-05	2.04	2.03	0.57	8.27	11.63
2005-06	2.20	2.22	1.61	7.13	14.63
2006-07	2.22	2.40	2.09	8.77	15.74
Average	1.72	2.48	1.77	7.42	9.67
S.D.	0.55	2.38	0.81	2.17	8.74
C.V. (%)	31.98	95.98	45.76	29.25	90.38

Source: Same as Table 6.8

Though, after so many years of the enactment of the IT Act, Internet banking has not gained satisfactory position yet increasing number of Internet banking using customers indicates the comparative popularity of it among various e-channels. Among various bank groups, new private sector banks and foreign banks are on the top position in providing more Internet banking services and their efficiency is also high as compared to other bank groups.

V
EMERGING ISSUES

New techniques brings with it some issues, if these issues are resolved efficiently then that technology can prove boon for that area. I-banking is not an exception. It has also bring with it some issues, like awareness regarding I-banking, covering rural and semi-urban area under I-banking, widening the scope of I-banking, transparency and security. These issues must be tackled very carefully and wisely to compete in the emerging global order.

Challenges in Internet Banking

Internet banking in India is in its earliest stage of development. Most of them are offering basic services only. Limited of banks are offering full services and of these most are private banks leading the market. The deregulation of banking industry coupled with the emergence of new banking technologies is enabling new competitors to enter the financial services market quickly and efficiently. Indian Internet banking faces following challenges:

Proper understanding of the customer: Proper identification of their needs and wants. For this a massive survey must be undertaken may be in collaboration with other banks.

- ***Need for transparency:*** In offering services as customers awareness has grown considerably.
- ***Breach of privacy:*** Online transactions enter straightaway into the records revealing the identity of customer. Thus black money cannot be transferred with ease.

- ***Bandwidth:*** Though companies claim to offer good speed and high bandwidth, still there are problems in accessing high speed on net. Internet banking can go high only on the wings of proper infrastructure comprising telecommunications and bandwidth.
- Computer literacy in India is still very low and that is a barrier in fast acceptance of Internet banking.
- The mindset of the Indian customer need to be changed.
- Customer has to be *protected against being "net-jacked" i.e.* he needs to be protected from fraud. Threats can be
  1. Cracking login and passwords is a common way of fiddling with the data.
  2. *Denial of services*: Directing millions of queries can block computer network.
  3. *Data Diddling*: Data can be modified in an unauthorised manner. A customer can therefore receive bills of higher amounts than the actual transactions.
  4. *Session hijacking*: Hijackers become unauthorised intermediaries between the server and the client; they can then hijack the data and prevent it from reaching the destination.

STRATEGIES WITH THEIR POSSIBLE SOLUTIONS TO MAKE I-BANKING MORE POPULAR

Awareness Regarding I-banking

It is imperative that more customers should be made aware of the service of Internet banking.

Possible Solutions

- Banks should provide operational knowledge of I-banking with each their functions.

- Banks should arrange demo-fares or provide information to customers at counters.
- Posters consisting list of services provided by internet banking should be displayed at appropriate places.

Rural and Semi-urban Sector: More than 60 per cent of the Indian population resides in rural areas. Therefore, it is need of the hour to capture this market through e-delivery channels. I-banking is the best alternative method in this direction. Hence, banks should make I-banking popular in rural and semi-urban areas too.

Possible Solution: Bank service providers should tie-up in this direction and try to provide Internet banking facility to rural population free of cost.

Wider Scope of Internet Banking

The banks should make the area of Internet banking wider by adding some more banking facilities. This will further strengthen the popularity of I-banking and help to earn more income.

Possible Solution: Banks should allow the cash transactions of small amount through I-banking.

Transparency

The banks should disclose the full information regarding service charges, service tax, interest, penalty if any, etc. to the customers to win their confidence.

Improvement of HRD Systems

The employees of e banks should be given training to match their skill with the requirements of changing environment. They should at least make them aware of all the schemes provided by the banks.

Possible Solutions

- Banks should conduct training to train their staff regarding 'how to use various e-channels' and update their knowledge in time to time.

- Arrangements should be made to take regular test of their employees (particularly Customer Care Executives) to test their knowledge.

Implication

The main implication of this paper is that i-banking is taking place in all bank groups but the speed is much higher in new private sector banks and foreign banks. The survival of the bank will depend up on the adoption of i-banking services, if the bank will not adopt i-banking that bank will out of the competition of their survival will become very difficult.

Future Studies

The study gives hint for comprehensive research in the following areas:

- Study of each channel and their impact on efficiency.
- Feassibility and viability of i-banking rural and semi-urban areas.
- Sex-wise use of i-banking.

Future Outlook

The findings of the present study predicts bright future of i-banking in India but their is an urgent need to spread awareness about i-banking particularly, in rural and semi-urban areas.

Conclusion

Internet banking is changing the banking industry and is having the major effects on banking relationships. The net banking, thus, "now is more of a norm rather than an exception in many developed countries" due to the fact that it is the economical way of providing banking services. Banking is now no longer confined to the traditional brick and mortar branches, where one has to be at the branch in person, to withdraw cash or deposit a cheque or request a statement of accounts. There is need to scan and analyse the market and respond to the needs of customers and to generate awareness regarding advantages of Internet banking. In true Internet banking, any inquiry or transaction is processed online without any reference to the branch (anywhere banking) at any time. Providing Internet banking is increasingly becoming a 'need to have' than a 'nice to have' services.

Thus Internet banking helps both, the customer as well as the bank, to lighten the burden of today's world and to save time, money and energy which is greatly required and appreciated.

REFERENCES

1. Arunachalam, L. and Sivasubramanian, M. (2007). 'The Future of Internet Banking in India', *Academic Open Internet Journal.* 20. Available online at: *www.acadjournal.com*
2. Avasthi, G.P. and Sharma, M. (2000-01). 'Information Technology in Banking: Challenges for Regulators'. *Prajanan.* XXIX(4). p. 17.
3. B. Janki (2002). 'Unleashing Employee Productivity: Need for a Paradigm Shift'. *Indian Banking Association Bulletin.* XXIV(3). March. 7-9.
4. Beer Stan (2006). Customers Preference on Internet Banking, Survey. Retrieved from *http://www.itwire.com/content/view/4570/53 on 20 March 2009.*
5. Booz, Allen, and Hamilton. (1997). *'Internet Banking: A Global Study of Potential'.* New York, NY: Booz Al-len & Hamilton Inc.
6. Dasgupta, P. (2002). Future of e-banking in India. Available online at: *www.projectshub.com*
7. Doll, W., Raghunathan, T., Lim, J., & Gupta, Y. (1995). 'A Confirmatory Analysis of the User Information Satisfaction Instrument'. *Information Systems Research.* 6(2). 177–188.
8. Gregory D. Williamson (2006). Enhanced Authentication In Online Banking , Journal of Economic Crime Management, Volume 4, Issue 2, Available online at: *http://www.utica.edu/academic/institutes/ecii/publications/articles/51D6D996-90F2-F468-AC09C4E8071575AE.pdf* on 18 March 2009.

9. Husain, F. (1988). *Computerisation and Mechanisation in Indian Banks* (New Delhi: Deep & Deep Publication).
10. Jayawardhena, C., and Foley, P. (2000). 'Changes in the Internet Banking Sector—The Case of Internet Banking in UK', Internet Research. *Electronic Networking Applications and Policy, 10*(1), 19-30.
11. Joseph, M., McClure, C. and Joseph, B. (1999). 'Service Quality in Banking Sector: The Impact of Technology on Service Delivery'. *International Journal of Bank Marketing.* 17(4).182–191.
12. Karjaluoto, H., Mattila, M., and Pento, T. (2002). 'Factors Underlying Attitude Formation Towards Online Internet Banking in Finland'. *International Journal of Bank Marketing.* 20(6). 261-272.
13. Khalil, M.N. and Pearson, J. M. (2007). 'The Influence of Trust on Internet Banking Acceptance'. *Journal of Internet Banking and Commerce. An Open Access Internet Journal.* 12(2). August. Available online at: http://www.arraydev.com/commerce/jibc/
14. Li, S., and Worthington, A.C. (2004). 'The Relationship Between the Adoption of Internet Banking and Electronic connectivity: An International Comparison'. *Discussion Paper, School of Economics and Fi-nance, Queensland University of Technology,* Brisbane QLD, Australia.
15. Malhotra, P. and Singh, B. (2006, October–December) 'The Impact of Internet Banking on Bank's Performance: the Indian experience'. *South Asian Journal of Management.* 13(4).
16. Mishra A. K. (NK) (2009). Internet Banking in India-Part I. Retrieved from *http://www.banknetindia.com/banking/ibkg.htm* on 18 March 2009.
17. Pikkarainen, T., Pikkarainen, K., Karjaluoto, H., & Pahnila, S. (2004). 'Consumer Acceptance of Online-banking: An Extension of the Technology Acceptance Model'. *Internet Research,* 14(3), 224–235.
18. Pathrose, P.P. (2001). 'Hi-tech. Banking Prospects and Problems', *IBA Bulletin.* XXIII(7). July.
19. Robinson, G. (2000). 'Bank to the Future'. *Internet Magazine.* Retrieved from *www.findarticles.com*
20. Rao, N.V. (2000). 'Changing Indian Banking Scenario: A Paradigm Shift'. *IBA Bulletin.* XXIV(1). 12-20.
21. Sathye, M. (1999). 'Adoption of Internet Banking by Australian Consumers: An Empirical Investigation'. *International Journal of Bank Marketing. 17*(7). 324-334.

22. Sohail, M. S., and Shanmugham, B. (2003). 'Internet Banking and Customer Preferences in Malaysia: An Empirical Investigation'. *Information Sciences.* 150(4). 207-217.

23. Shastri, R.V. (2001). 'Technology for Banks in India—Challenges'. *IBA Bulletin.* XXIII(3). March.

24. Suganthi, B., Balachandher, S., & Balachandran, K.G. (2001). Internet Banking Patronage: An Empirical Investigation of Malaysia. *Journal of International Banking and Commerc.*6(1). Available online at: *http://www.arraydev.com/commerce/JIBC/0103_01.htm*

25. Vageesh, N.S. (2000), 'New Private Banks: New Kids on the Block'. *Business Line.* March.

26. Vijayan, P. and Shanmugam, Bala (2003). 'Service Quality Evaluation of Internet Banking in Malaysia'. *Journal of Internet Banking and Commerce.* 8(1). June.

CHAPTER 7

A Theory-based Model for the Study of Internet Banking Adoption by the Bank Executives

—MR. MANORANJAN DASH

ABSTRACT

The forces of economic change, tied with advancements in technology, prompt banks to rethink their use of traditional branches and begin forming new partnerships to deliver financial services. The Internet seems to be the new delivery channel in the banking sector. Factors such as the security and trust have been identified by previous studies as the determinants of Internet banking adoption. The study enhances the technology acceptance model (TAM) with an additional construct of social influence (SI). Data are collected from executives of public and private sector banks. A total of 300 questionnaires are distributed using purposive sampling method. A structural model was proposed and tested, examining the important factors as well as social influence on the use of Internet banking by bank executives. The proposed model serves as a base for comparison with other models. The results of this study also indicate that perceived usefulness (PU) and perceived ease of use (PEOU) are also the important factors which influence the use of Internet banking by bank executives. In addition, social factors have strong and positive influence on adoption of Internet banking.

Keywords

Internet Banking, Social influence, Consumer Behaviour.

Introduction

In the arouse of the Internet revolution, electronic commerce emerged and allowed businesses to interact more effectively with their customers and other corporations. In this proliferated digital age, banking industry has been using this new communication channel to reach its varieties of customers. Electronic commerce has become a very important technological advancement for businesses by changing business practices (*Brodie et al.*, 2007; (*Gonza'lez et al.*, 2008; *Lichtenstein* and Williamson, 2006). This has experienced tremendous growth in recent years as a result of new business initiatives utilising these technologies (*Barwise* and *Farley*, 2005). In particular, industries that are information-oriented such as banking services and securities trading sector are expected to experience the highest growths in e-commerce (*Ibrahim et al.* 2006; *Hughes*, 2002). Undoubtedly, Internet banking has experienced explosive growth and has transformed traditional practices in banking (*Barwise* and *Farley*, 2005; *Gonzalez et al.*, 2008; *Lichtenstein* and *Williamson*, 2006). The banking industry as declared information privacy and security to be major obstacles in the development of consumer related electronic commerce. Besides that, success of banking industry depends on the capabilities of management to anticipate and react to such changes in the financial marketplace (*Gan et al.*, 2006). Meanwhile Internet banking also allows customer to have direct access to their financial information and to undertake financial transactions with more convenient way (*Rotchanakitumnuai* and *Speece*, 2003). For the success of most banks, it has become paramount to attract existing bank customers to adopt the options of Internet banking. This creates huge cost savings by means of scale effects in bank operations (*Chen* and *Hitt*, 2002). *Rao* and *Prathima* (2003) provided a theoretical analysis of Internet banking in India, and found that as compared to the banks abroad, Indian banks offering online services still have a long way to go. For online banking to reach a critical mass, there has to be sufficient number of users and the sufficient infrastructure in place. Various authors have found that Internet banking is fast becoming popular in India (*Gupta,* 1999; *Pegu,* 2000; *Dasgupta,* 2002). However, it is still in its evolutionary stage. In India, comparatively less number of studies has been conducted on the current status of Internet banking and customer satisfaction compared to other countries. Thus, there is a lot of scope for the research to present new ideas concerning Internet banking in India which may be useful to the Indian banking industry.

RESEARCH OBJECTIVES

1. To understand the behaviour of bank executives regarding use of Internet banking.
2. To assess the social influence on acceptance and use of Internet banking.

REVIEW OF LITERATURE

The Technology Acceptance Model (TAM), developed by Davis *et al.* (1989), is one of the most widely used and influential models in the field of information systems, technology and services. It has been fully validated to be powerful as a framework to predict user acceptance of new technology. TAM extended the theory of reasoned action (TRA) (*Fishbein* and *Ajzen,* 1980) by introducing two belief factors, perceived usefulness and perceived ease of use, which substitute for many of TRA's attitude measure. These two factors are postulated to determine an individual's intention to use a technology-based system with intention to use playing the role of mediator of actual system use. Perceived ease of use is also posited to have a direct impact on perceived usefulness. In general, TAM is able to explain up to 40 per cent of the variance in usage intentions and 30 per cent in system usage (*Meister* and *Compeau,* 2002). To increase the predictive power of TAM, it was suggested to consider the role of external variables (*Davis,* 1993). Legris *et al.* (2003) also noted the critical importance of examining external variables, since they are the ultimate drivers for the use of technology. In a variety of disciplines, external variables that were used to explore the effect on technology usage are individual differences, such as cognitive, personality, demographic, and situational variables. (*Zumd,* 1979). An abundance of related studies on TAM also found a significant relationship between individual differences and technology acceptance (*Hubona* and *Kennick*, 1996; *Jackson et al.,* 1997; *Agarwal* and *Prasad*, 1999; *Venkatesh*, 2000; *Venkatesh* and *Morris*, 2000; *Burton-Jones* and *Hubona*, 2006). The TAM tends to predict user adoption of new technologies in positive perspective. However, customers will reduce their usage or even refuse to use a technology if they subjectively expect that an injury or a loss likely occurs while using the technology. The degrees of risk that consumers perceive and their risk tolerance are attitudinal factors that affect their usage (*Chan et al.,* 2004). Perceived risk has multi-dimensions, including financial, performance, physical, psychological, social and time risks (*Jacoby* and *Kaplan*, 1972; *Havlena* and *DeSarbo*, 1990; *Murray* and *Schlacter*, 1990; *Stone* and *Gronhaug*, 1993). There is very little research to compare the effect of social influence (SI) on technology usage behaviour. Critiques of TAM and related theories have also suggested that the model has strong limitations in terms of SI. Legris reviewed 22 articles published from 1980 to 2001 that used TAM and concluded that TAM was a useful model, but it lacks the variables associated with social change processes (Stam, Stanton, Guzman, 2005). This criticism suggested that in absence of SI the explanatory power of TAM is limited despite its statistical success of its regression models. SI can be defined as "the degree to which an individual perceives that important others believe he or she should use the new system". The role of SI in technology acceptance issues are complex and subject to a wide range of contingent influences. (*Venkatesh* and *Morris*, 2000). Social elements exerted profound effects on the performance of employees with the introduction of new technology. New technology affects the social organisation of work, access to resources and organisational structures. The construct SI has been incorporated from the model of TRA, Personal Computing Utilisation (PCU) and from Innovation Diffusion Theory (IDT) (*Srite*, 2006). As technology advances, new systems have been introduced and users find more alternatives to use the technology. While users are inclined to use some specific technology, their reference groups might influence by suggesting to choose a certain alternative. Hence, the dimension of SI might be an important factor while conducting research on adoption of technology (*Kim*, *Jhang* and *Lee*, 2006). The construct of SI had a similar impact in the TAM relationships as it did in TPB (*Morris*, *Venkatesh*, *Ackerman* 2005). The foundation of Social Influence in TAM was originated from subjective norm as described in TRA. Subjective norm was included as a direct determinant of behavioural intention in TRA and then in TPB. The reasoning for a direct effect of SI on intention is that people may choose to perform a behaviour even if they are not favourable towards that behaviour or its consequences. If they believe one or more important referents think that they should use the computers, they are sufficiently motivated to act in accordance with the referents. Taylor and Todd (1995) examined a direct significant effect on intention to use. Davis, Bagozzi and Warshaw (1989) found that SI had no significant effect on intention to use and therefore it has been omitted from the original TAM, but need for additional research to investigate the impact of social influence over intention to use was emphasised continuously. (*Venkatesh*, *Morris*, and *Davis*, 2003). SI had a positive effect on intention to use IT only when system use is mandatory. They also found that SI had a positive direct effect on PU. Angst and Agarwal (2004) observed the effect of SI by including a multiple process of compliance, identification and internalization and found that individuals were influenced by SI while using IT. Song and Kim (2006) observed that SI has a very little effect on technology usage behavior. But he emphasised to include this construct in the TAM model. On the basis of above studies, it is hypothesised that SI will affect the intention to use the Internet banking.

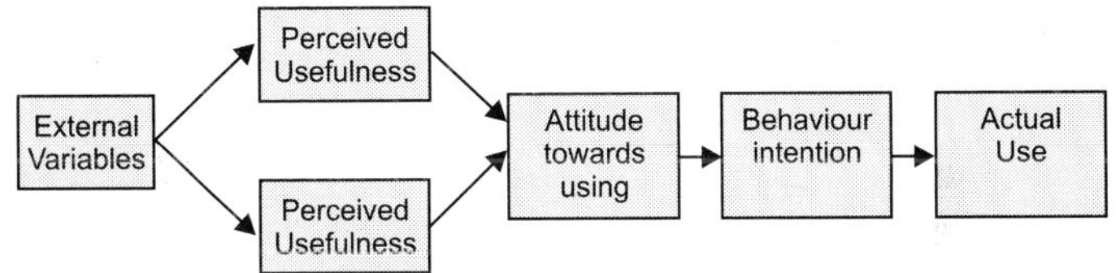

Fig. 7.1. Technology Acceptance Model (*Source:* Davis , 1993 p.476)

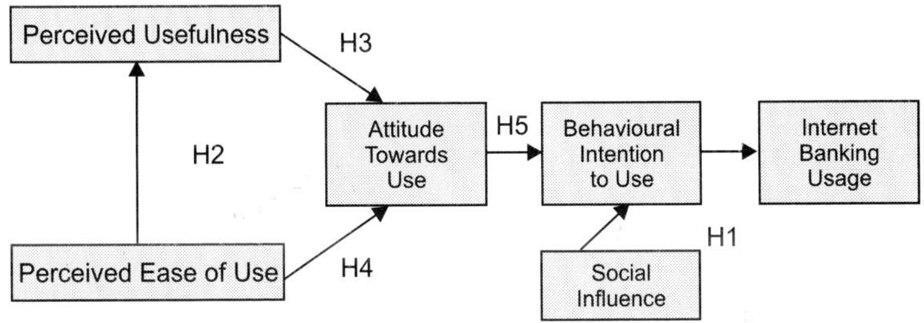

(PROPOSED RESEARCH MODEL)

Research Methodology and Analysis

A total of 300 responses were received. We collected data from bank employees in Odisha who use internet banking. The questionnaire developed for TAM by Davis (1989)—adapting the scales for Perceived Usefulness and Perceived Ease of Use. We tested the structural model by means of Confirmatory Factor Analysis (CFA). An exploratory factor analysis using SPSS was conducted on the survey data. A seven-point likert scale ranging from (1) 'strongly disagree' to (7) 'strongly agree' were used to assess responses. The measurement models specify how hypothetical constructs are measured in terms of the observed variables. Furthermore, the structural model specifies causal relationships among the latent variables. It is employed to describe the causal effects and amount of unexplained variance (*Anderson* and *Gerbing*, 1982). Structural Equation Modelling (SEM) was applied to evaluate the strength of the hypothesised relationships among the constructs in the theoretical model developed by this study. Basically, SEM is a family of statistical techniques that incorporates and integrates factor analysis and path analysis. It can be utilized to model multivariate casual relationships and to test multivariate hypotheses. SEM model building consists of a two-stage process (*Jöreskog*, and *Sörbom*, 1993; *Hoyle*, 1995; *Hair et al.*, 1998; *Maruyama*, 1998), in which the measurement models are tested before testing the structural model. Confirmatory factor analysis (CFA) is conducted to assess the reliability and validity of the measurement model, whereas the structural model is analysed to evaluate the strength of the relationships among constructs hypothesised in the research model.

H1: Perceived Social Influence will positively influence the behavioral intention to Internet banking.

H2: Customer's perceived ease of use has a significant impact on his/her perceived usefulness of Internet banking.

H3: Customer's perceived usefulness has a positive impact on his/her attitude towards using Internet banking.

H4: Customer's perceived ease of use has a positive impact on his/her attitude towards using Internet banking.

H5: Customer's attitude towards using Internet banking has a significant impact on his/her intention to use it.

Measurement Model Analysis

Both, the R^2 and the path coefficients indicate how well the model is performing. R^2 shows the predictive power of the model, and the values should be interpreted in the same way as R^2 in a regression analysis. Partial Least Squares (PLS), an implementation of structural equation modelling (SEM) was used to test the model and analyse the factors that affect customers attitude towards Internet banking acceptance. Moreover, this approach was chosen because of its ability to test causal relationships between constructs with multiple measurement items (*Jöreskog* and *Sörbom*,1993).

Results for the Research Path Tests

Research Path	R^2	Path coefficient (β)	P-Value
SI ⟶ BI	0.316	0.690	0.000***
PEOU ⟶ PU	0.594	0.784	0.000***
PU ⟶ ATT	0.694	0.792	0.000***
PEOU ⟶ ATT	0.589	0.782	0.000***
ATT ⟶ BI	0.669	0.876	0.000***

*** p< 0.0001

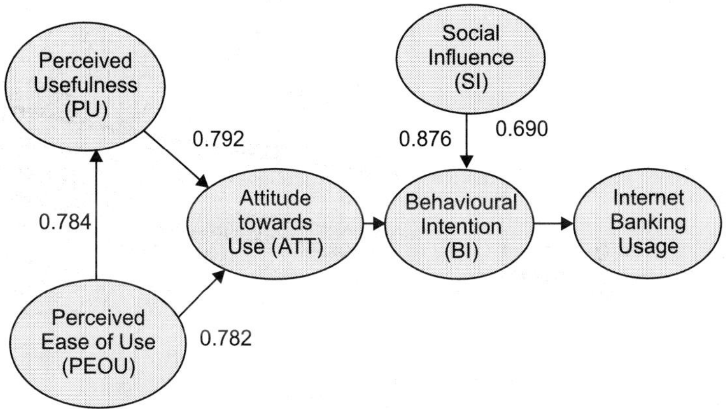

(Results of Structural Equation Model)

It was found that awareness of Internet banking services and its benefits explains 63 per cent of the variance in perceived usefulness (PU). The paths had positive effect, with path coefficient of 0.792. Meaning, hypotheses 3 was supported. Perceived Social Influence have significant effects on Behavioural Intention to Internet Banking (BI) and together explain 67 per cent of the variance. These two factors had positive path coefficients that hypotheses 4 and 5 were also supported. Perceived ease of use (PEOU) and perceived usefulness (PU) influenced customer attitudes towards using Internet banking, supporting hypotheses 3 and 4. Theses factors had positive path coefficients Attitudes towards (ATT) use explain 73 per cent of the variance in adoption intention (AI) with path coefficients of 0.876. As a result, hypothesis 5 was also supported.

Conclusion

The results support the view that Perceived Ease of Use and Social Influence are predicting variables, affecting Perceived Usefulness and Attitude as intervening variables, and Intention to Use internet banking as the dependent variable. Perceived Usefulness and Perceived Social Influence has a direct effect on Intention, while Perceived Ease of Use has only an indirect impact. The results of hypotheses testing provide satisfactory support for the extended TAM through the SEM analysis. The research model was based on an extension of the technology acceptance model with incorporating constructs of social influence The findings provide useful insight for bank management in developing appropriate marketing strategies to meet bank executives demands, and further to retain and expand customer base.

REFERENCES

1. Byrne, B.M., 2001. Structural Equation Modelling with AMOS, Basic Concepts, Applications, and Programming, Multivariate Applications Series. Lawrence Erlbaum Associates, Hillsdale, New Jersey.
2. Chan, S.C. and Lu, M. T., 2004. Understanding Internet Banking Adoption and Use Behaviour: a Hong Kong Perspective. *Journal of Global Information Management,* 12, 21-43.
3. Chau, P. Y. K., 1997. Reexamining a Model for Evaluating Information Center Success Using a Structural Equation Modelling Approach. Decision Sciences, 28, 309-335.
4. Chin, W.W. and Todd, P.A., 1995. On the Use, Usefulness, and Ease of Use of Structural Equation Modelling in MIS Research: A Note of Caution. *MIS Quarterly,* 19, 237-246.
5. Cohen, J., 1988. Statistical Power Analysis for the Behavioural Sciences, 2nd Edition, Lawrence Erlbaum Associates, Hillsdale, New Jersey.

6. Cornwell, T.B., Roy, D.P. and Steinard II, E.A., 2001. Exploring Managers' Perceptions of the Impact of Sponsorship on Brand Equity. *Journal of Advertising,* 30, 41-51.

7. Davis F.D., Bagozzi R.P. and Warshaw P.R., 1989. User Acceptance of Computer Technology : A Comparison of Two Theoretical Models. *Management Science,* 35, 982-1003.

8. Davis, F. D., 1989. Perceived Usefulness, Perceived Ease of Use, and User Acceptance of Information Technology. *MIS Quarterly,* 13, 319-336. 23

9. Fishbein, M.A. and Ajzen, I., 1975. *Belief, Intention and Behaviour: An introduction to Theory and Research.* Addison-Wesley, Reading, Massachusetts.

10. Gefen, D., Karahanna, E. and Straub, D. W., 2003. Trust and TAM in Online Shopping: An Integrated Model. *MIS Quarterly,* 27, 51-90.

11. Hair, J., R. Anderson, Tatham, R. and Black, W., 1998. *Multivariate Data Analysis.* Prentice Hall, New Jersey.

12. Hendrickson, A.R., Massey, P.D. and Cronan, T.P., 1993. On the Test-retest Reliability of Perceived Usefulness and Perceived Ease of Use Scales. *MIS Quarterly,* 17, 227-230.

13. Jarvenpaa, S.L. and Todd, P.A., 1997. Consumer Reactions to Electronic Shopping on the World Wide Web. *International Journal of Electronic Commerce*, 1, 59-88.

14. Agarwal, R. and Prasad, J. 1999. Are Individual Differences Germane to the Acceptance of New Information Technologies. *Decision Sciences,* 30(2): 361–391.

15. Bagozzi, R.P. and Yi, Y. 1988. On the Evaluation of Structural Equation Model. *Journal of Academy of Marketing Science,* 16: 74–94.

16. Chan, S.C. and Lu, M.T. 2004. Understanding Internet Banking Adoption and Use Behaviour: a Hong Kong Perspective. *Journal of Global Information Management,* 12 (3), July-September: 21–43.

17. Chang, T.Y. 2003. *Dynamics of Banking Technology Adoption: An Application to Internet Banking.* Department of Economics, Coventry: University of Warwick.

18. Cheng, T.C.E, Lam, D.Y.C. and Yeung, A.C.L. 2006. Adoption of Internet Banking: An Empirical Study in Hong Kong. *Decision Support Systems,* 42: 1558–1572.

19. Chung, W. and Paynter, J. 2002. An Evaluation of Internet Banking in New Zealand. *Proceedings of the 35th Annual Hawaii International Conference on System Sciences,* January, HICSS-35.

20. Eriksson, K., Kerem, K., Nilsson, D. 2005. Customer Acceptance of Internet Banking in Estonia. *International Journal of Bank Marketing,* 23(2): 200–216.

21. Jaruwachirathanakul, B. and Fink, S. 2005. Internet Banking Adoption Strategies for a Development Country: The Case of Thailand. *Internet Research,* 15 (3): 295–311.

22. Maruyama, G.M. 1998. Basics of Structural Equation Modelling, Thousand Oaks, CA: Sage Publications.

23. Meister, D.B., and Compeau, D.R. 2002. Infusion of Innovation Adoption: An Individual Perspective. *Annual Conference of the Administrative Sciences Association of Canada* (ASAC), May 25–28, Winnipeg, Manitoba: 23–33.

24. Ndubisi, N.O., Gupta, O.K. and Ndubisi, G.C. 2005. The Moguls Model of Computing; Integrating the Moderating Impact of Users' Persona into the Technology Acceptance Model. *Journal of Global Information Technology Management,* 8(1): 27–47.

25. Sathye, M. 1999. Adoption of Internet Banking by Australian Consumers: An Empirical Investigation. *International Journal of Bank Marketing,* 17(7): 324–334.

26. Stone, R.N. and Gronhaug, K. 1993. Perceived Risk: Further Considerations for the Marketing Discipline. *European Journal of Marketing,* 27(3): 39–50.

27. Tan, M. and Teo, T. 2000. Factors Influencing the Adoption of Internet Banking. *Journal of the Association for Information Systems,* 1(5): 1–42.

Appendix–1. Reliability Analysis

Constructs	Items	Loading	Composite Reliability	Cronbach's alpha(α)
Social Influence(SI)	SI 1	0.779	0.817	0.865
	SI 2	0.654		
	SI 3	0.965		
	SI 4	0.871		
Perceived Ease of use (PEOU)	PEOU 1	0.818	0.912	0.876
	PEOU 2	0.813		
	PEOU 3	0.798		
	PEOU 4	0.867		
Perceived Usefulness (PU)	PU 1	0.982	0.945	0.887
	PU 2	0.932		
	PU 3	0.894		
	PU 4	0.821		
Attitude Towards Use (ATT)	ATT 1	0.786	0.872	0.813
	ATT 2	0.795		
	ATT 3	0.812		
	ATT 4	0.654		
Behavioural Intention To Use (BI)	BI 1	0.956	0.921	0.868
	BI 2	0.978		
	BI 3	0.872		

CHAPTER 8

Higher Education Opportunities for Foreign Participation in India
An Overview

—DR. T. MUTHAIYEN
—DR. A. ABDUL RAHEEM

ABSTRACT

This paper provides an overview of the Indian higher education system, with a special focus on the current status and possibilities of foreign participation in the sector. Section I presents a brief introduction to higher education in India today. Section II discusses important systemic challenges in the sector, specifically problems of insufficient access, disparities between social groups and regions, and quality control. These problems stem from the lack of public investment and a flawed regulatory structure. The most noticeable result of these deficiencies has been the rapid and unregulated growth of private provision. Section III focuses on the prospects for foreign education providers in India. It maps the existing government view of foreign and private participation and argues that the regulatory framework, by imposing high costs on institutions, tends to drive out legitimate actors and attract those interested in short-term gains. It also attempts to show that there has been an increasing discussion within government circles on the role foreign institutions could play, and that this signals a growing public debate that can be successfully leveraged by potential foreign entrants. Strategies for doing so are touched upon. Section IV discusses the Canadian experience and offers recommendations for Canadian actors. It emphasises the importance of having the correct perspective on the future of higher education in a rapidly globalising world, and describes possible ways in which Canadian actors can set the stage for meaningful collaboration with Indian institutions. Section V concludes by briefly arguing that in the final analysis, foreign participation hinges on the regulatory system's ability to successfully balance two conflicting objectives—building a world-class educational system, and ensuring that education remains a charitable activity that embodies national values and priorities.

Introduction

India currently has the world's largest number of higher education institutions, and the third-largest student population. Most recent estimates place the number of institutions at about 18,000 and the number of students at more than 11 million. Behind these numbers are six decades of phenomenal growth, initially fuelled by public investment but lately attributable to a greater extent to the unabated growth of the private sector. Since 1990, the number of institutions has been growing at an annual rate of 6 per cent, yet this has not kept pace with the demand for higher education. More importantly, growth of good quality institutions has been negligible. As a result, Indian higher education has often been characterised as a sea of mediocrity containing only a few islands of excellence. Equity is an additional concern. Socially and economically disadvantaged groups are under-represented in the system and their educational attainments tend to be below average.

The key problems of access, equity and quality are but symptoms of a deeper malaise. There are two primary constraints affecting the system today—the decline of public investment in higher education, and the existence of a flawed, overly rigid and ineffective regulatory framework. These problems have steered higher education into previously uncharted waters, namely privatisation and foreign participation. These developments have been spurred also by changes in the global trade regime and the education sectors of other nations. In this sense, India's education system is at a crossroads. It is yet unclear whether the government can successfully manage the system, thereby making the most of India's much vaunted demographic and educational advantages. As for nations interested in penetrating the Indian education market, this is the time to carefully observe developments in the legal and regulatory regimes, particularly with reference to emerging ideological differences on the issue of foreign participation in higher education.

Systemic Challenges in Higher Education

Access

In 2001, about 35 per cent of India's population was aged 14 or under. Based on the current burgeoning demand for basic education and a 20 per cent gross graduation ratio at the upper secondary level, the projected 'demographic dividend' is poised to put considerable pressure on the higher education system in the coming years. Although estimates vary, the Gross Enrolment Ratio (GER) in higher education has been estimated at somewhere between 7 per cent and 11 per cent. While this makes India better off than many South Asian and Sub-Saharan African countries, it does not compare favourably with countries such as Egypt (35%), Turkey (31%), Brazil (24%), Iran (24%), China (20%), South Africa (15%), and of course Canada (62%), the United States (83%) and the Republic of Korea (91%). The data both globally and within India suggest that a high per capita income is positively correlated with a high GER. While the direction of causality cannot be conclusively established in this study, it is sufficient to note that the evidence supports theories that emphasise the importance of human capital to long-term economic growth, and the need to channel the benefits of economic growth into investments in human capital. Thus one of the primary objectives of the system at the moment is to expand access to higher education in order to meet growing demand. However, it is important to note that expanding access is not equivalent to expanding supply. A broader conception of 'access' is required, one that emphasises inter alias the need for expanding the supply of *good quality* institutions. Of course, this measure alone will not necessarily ensure that higher education reaches every person that desires it.

Equity

There are three main axes of disparity that exist in the domain of higher education in India—gender, caste, and region. All three become important when considering a strategy to expand access. The enrolment of women in higher education is traditionally measured by the Gender Parity Index (GPI), which is a ratio of female GER to male GER. The 2005 GPI, compiled from Census and University Grants Commission (UGC) data, was estimated at 0.75. When compared to a relevant-age population ratio of 0.91 (*i.e.* female population aged 18-24 as a ratio of male population aged 18-24), it appears that women are significantly under-represented in higher education. It is especially pertinent that the GPI throughout school (grades 1 to 12) is 0.91. This suggests a tendency for women to drop out of the education system after grade 12, possibly due to various social pressures.

Inequalities of caste (and tribe) are also significant. Constitutionally designated disadvantaged groups—Scheduled Castes (SC) and Scheduled Tribes (ST)—are under-represented, and consistently under-perform relative to their peers. Compared to the overall GER of the country (7%-11%), the GER for SCs is 6.7 per cent and for STs 4.9 per cent. Although various government schemes exist to subsidize the education of students from these groups, few efforts have been made to systematically look at student achievement in order to determine the effectiveness of these schemes. Nonetheless, the issue of under-representation remains important. In this context, it is worth noting overlapping disadvantages. For instance, while the overall GPI for India stands at 0.75, the GPI among SC students is 0.64, and among ST students 0.55. Thus women in these disadvantaged categories are considerably less likely to participate in the higher education system than women in general.

Lastly, regional inequalities in higher education highlight the uneven nature of growth in the sector over the last few years. Approximately 58 per cent of all higher education institutions are located in six States—Uttar Pradesh, Andhra Pradesh, Maharashtra, Karnataka, Madhya Pradesh and Tamil Nadu—which are also among the ten most populated states of India. This geographic concentration reflects the considerable growth of institutions in South and West India relative to other regions. Variation also exists in terms of enrolment, with the GER across States and Union Territories ranging from 26 per cent in Chandigarh to 4 per cent in Arunachal Pradesh. Similarly, in the case of gender parity, states and Union Territories such as Goa, Chandigarh, Kerala, Delhi, Punjab and Pondicherry are all relatively more favourable to women, whereas women are most disadvantaged in the States of Bihar, Arunachal Pradesh, Jharkhand, Orissa and Rajasthan. All of the above, and other regional data within India, suggest significant imbalances in the capacity and sophistication of systems for higher education between the South and West on the one hand, and the North, East and North-East on the other.

Quality

Quality is a critical factor in the assessment of a higher education system. It can be measured externally according to pre-defined institutional parameters, or by simply looking at the educational and job market outcomes of an institution's graduates. Institutional assessments are carried out by two accreditation agencies in India—the National Assessment and Accreditation Council (NAAC) and the National Board of Accreditation (NBA). The former, an affiliate of the University Grants Commission (UGC), deals with colleges offering general education; the latter, an affiliate of the All India Council for Technical Education (AICTE), deals with professional and technical colleges. Below is a brief analysis of data from the NAAC.

Although the NAAC covers not more than 3500 colleges (roughly one-fifth of India's colleges), its grading system provides a useful insight into quality across the country. A simplified scale encompassing two former grading systems (in use from 1998-2002 and 2002-2007) shows that as of 2006-2007, only 28 per cent of NAAC accredited colleges had received an above average grade while 47 per cent got a below average grade, and 25 per cent were rated. The grading system employs a holistic set of measurement tools that evaluate most important aspects of an institution. It is of some concern that most colleges are not assessed above the average grade.

Another indicator of quality is the academic performance of the students of a college. In this regard, the UGC collects data on the number of students passing their final exams in graduate and post-graduate courses in all the colleges it recognizes. The data for 2002 are alarming. For instance, amongst all the students appearing for final examinations in Commerce, only 56 per cent passed. Similarly, only 49 per cent passed in Computer Science/Applications, 61 per cent in Science and 61 per cent in Management. Performance was relatively better in Engineering (79%), Medicine (75%), Nursing (97%) and Education (89.5%). Overall for 2002, only 63 per cent of the students taking final exams in all disciplines passed. These figures bear out the adage that quantity does not necessarily imply quality.

If exam results are not entirely convincing, we might look at the labour market performance of graduates. Although not much information is publicly available, a small dataset on recent engineering graduates from a handful of Indian states was published by the Institute for Applied Manpower Research (IAMR) in 2005. The survey shows that, surprisingly, states such as Kerala, Uttar Pradesh and West Bengal are attractive job markets for degree-holders in the major sub-disciplines of Engineering, whereas states with a proliferation of engineering colleges like Andhra Pradesh, Karnataka and Tamil Nadu have relatively lower rates of employment for students with the same qualifications. Prima facie, this suggests that a regulatory environment that promotes the large scale expansion of colleges is less effective (or discerning) in keeping out low quality institutions, thus leading to the production of a large number of relatively non-employable graduates. The data also show that diploma holders in Engineering are much less likely to succeed in the job market than degree holders. This is particularly relevant given that in 2003, 60 per cent of engineering graduates were diploma holders.

Public Investment

The problems of access, equity and quality stem in part from a lack of public funding for higher education. Public institutions without adequate funds to hire good faculty, offer scholarships to disadvantaged groups and expand enrolment, are finding it harder to meet growing demand. It took the politics of caste to give an impetus to public spending in the 11th Plan. The government injected a substantial amount into higher education, not to improve quality but to increase the number of minority places, allowing for the implementation of the government's own quota for Other Backward Castes (OBCs) in Central Universities and institutions. Despite this recent politically motivated action, the State continues to gradually withdraw from higher education.

The government currently spends about 3.7 per cent of GDP on education. While this is higher than countries such as Indonesia, Cameroon, Gambia, it is lower than Brazil,

Mexico, Iran, Botswana, Uganda and other developing nations, let alone most of the developed economies of Europe and North America. In India, higher education has received less public support than lower levels. In 2005-2006, university and technical education only accounted for about 15 per cent of total spending on education by central and state governments. Between 1990-1991 and 2004-2005, the share of GDP spent on higher education fell from 0.77 per cent to 0.66 per cent, whereas the share dedicated to primary education rose from 1.78 per cent to 1.89 per cent. When calculated per student, this amounts to a 28 per cent real term decline between 1990-1991 and 2002-2003. All these data show that government (at Centre and State levels) is not investing enough in higher education, and that over the last two decades, spending levels have been falling. Moreover, the funds poured into the system every year cover mostly non-program expenses, most of which are salaries. In 2004-2005, capital expenditure accounted for only 1.84 per cent of total education expenditure by State Education Departments. With funds drying up from the Center, there is little money to finance the growth and development of higher education in the states.

Privatisation

As a result of the government's gradual withdrawal from higher education, the private sector has begun to play an increasingly important role. In less than a decade, it has filled the space recently vacated by the public sector and transformed the education landscape—particularly professional and technical education. Indeed in one short year, between 2003-2004 and 2004-2005, the total number of institutions in the system shot up by 12%. Given the lack of public investment, it is safe to assume that most of these were private institutions. UGC data on recognised colleges show that 20 per cent of the country's 17,000 colleges are privately owned and funded, while 37 per cent of the colleges are privately owned but receive some form of aid from the government. Levels of privatisation vary across major States, ranging from 63 per cent of colleges being private and unaided in Andhra Pradesh, to 9.3 per cent in Haryana. Private providers have been eager to step into areas for which there is verifiable market demand, thus justifying the higher fees charged to students who expect higher incomes upon graduation. Students, on the other hand, are increasingly enrolling in professional courses that make them more competitive in the labour market, and they are willing to pay higher fees for this. Supply from the private sector appears to be meeting the rising demand in the face of declining public investment.

Below the surface, the situation is more complex. Private providers, in the interest of maximizing profit, have every incentive to 'minimise costs' by compromising on the quality of the education provided. Although the better known private players (*e.g.* Amity, NIIT, Aptech) are careful to protect their reputation, the majority of private colleges and universities are not known for their scrupulous academic standards. The relatively poorer education delivered by the private sector is reflected in the growing scarcity of employable graduates in the technical and professional fields, a fact highlighted by the NASSCOM-McKinsey study of 2005. Related to the possible compromise of academic standards is the issue of unfair trade practices. Private providers have used the tight supply of higher education to maximise income through unorthodox means such as the imposition of 'capitation fees', misrepresentation of courses and corruption in admissions practices. Methods such as these ultimately harm the interests of students. From time to time, the government and the judiciary have taken steps to regulate these practices, but government regulation and judicial intervention are often muddled, overly complex and counter-productive.

The Regulatory Framework

The State has a clear role to play in higher education. India's intervention in this regard has been less than ideal. The most fundamental flaw lies in the institutional architecture of the UGC itself. It is the sole authority on almost all regulatory matters in the university system, including access (fees and admissions), finance (funds disbursal), quality (accreditation via the NAAC) and entry into the market (the conferral of degree-granting powers). In essence, the UGC is a super-regulator. Instead of a regulatory framework that provides incentives to promote academic excellence, the UGC is a discretionary and highly centralised structure that discourages academic innovation, promotes standardisation over standards, and is not responsive to the dynamics of academia in the various disciplines.

This form of regulation imposes significant costs on the system, exacerbating existing constraints on public investment. For instance, the requirement that every university, at central or state level, can only be set up through specific legislation not only presents a significant barrier to entry but also raises the public cost of establishing a new university. The judiciary has also contributed to the muddle of policies and regulations currently in existence. Often brought into the picture when the legislature or executive has abdicated its responsibilities, the judiciary's rulings have sent mixed signals to stakeholders. In a series of judgments from 1992 to 2005, the Supreme Court vacillated on the issue of autonomy in fee setting and admissions for private and minority-run institutions, once reversing a previous ruling and in another instance, having to issue a new judgment to clarify its position. During this period, the Court seems to have abandoned previous suspicions regarding the financing of education and private providers. Yet on issues of access (especially caste-based quotas) and minority rights, the Court has remained ambivalent, possibly due to the political sensitivities involved. On the whole, there has been little clarity from the Supreme Court on its views pertaining to access, equity and privatisation in this domain.

The result has been the *de facto* privatisation of higher education. While the Courts and regulatory agencies have been reluctant to acknowledge the importance of private investment as a supplement to public funds, the market has ignored them and continued growing. Regulators have been caught off-guard, failing to grasp the full import of this new dynamic or to develop the needed management tools. Meanwhile, system insiders who understand the possibilities of private investment have used it to their advantage. It has been argued that political parties of all stripes have permitted privatisation because they recognise the potential of private funding as an effective (and costless) way to alleviate the current "fiscal exhaustion" of public budgets, to accommodate the new quota regime, or to act as a new (and more abundant) source of patronage. Ultimately, the UGC and AICTE will need to develop a coherent body of regulation for the private sector that recognises its growing role in the financing of higher education but also holds it accountable to standards of academic excellence and equitable access. Until then, institutions and students will continue to bear the brunt of an uneasy relationship between the public and the private sector.

Foreign Participation

Regulation of foreign education providers has evolved in similar ways to the regulation of private providers. Despite overt distrust at the outset, regulators have gradually given their approval to some institutions, but have imposed conditions. This section outlines the regulatory landscape for foreign participants and briefly discusses the current situation before outlining strategies open to would-be entrants in the market.

The Regulatory Landscape for Foreign Participation

In the new millennium, two simultaneous processes have shaped the regulatory landscape facing interested foreign parties—first, the rapid privatisation of higher education, and second, the growing importance of the international trade regime under the World Trade Organisation (WTO) and the General Agreement on Trade in Services (GATS). Following the lead of other nations that have moved quickly to safeguard their domestic education systems, Indian legislators and policymakers recognised the need for national legislation and policies governing foreign entry into the domestic arena. However, the government's response has been hasty and heavy-handed. Rather than making an ally of the market, regulation has created significant barriers to the entry and operations of potential private and foreign providers of higher education.

A host of regulations, policy documents and pending or withdrawn legislation provides insights on current thinking among policymakers and legislators grappling with the issue of foreign participation. The most important and relevant regulations are :

1. UGC (Establishment and Maintenance of Standards in Private Universities) Regulations 2003—*currently active.*
2. AICTE Regulations for Entry and Operation of Foreign Universities / Institutions Imparting Technical Education in India, 2005—*currently active.*
3. The Private Universities (Establishment and Regulation) Bill 1995—*withdrawn from Parliament in the 2007 Monsoon Session.*
4. The Private Professional Educational Institutions (Regulation of Admission and Fixation of Fee) Bill 2005–*pending (status unknown).*

The Foreign Educational Institutions (Regulation of Entry and Operation, Maintenance of Quality and Prevention of Commercialisation) Bill 2007—*yet to be introduced in Parliament.* These regulations taken as a whole reflect the distrust and fear of private (and foreign) enterprise that permeate India's educational bureaucracy. Private/foreign institutions are typically required to clear numerous administrative hurdles before being granted approval. For instance, the AICTE has a mandatory application procedure for foreign institutions that requires submissions to pass from the AICTE to an ad hoc Standing

Committee, then an ad hoc Expert Committee, then a Sub-Committee of the Expert Committee, and then back to the AICTE before final approval is granted. Applicants must also provide a security deposit of an amount not specified in the regulations. Aside from erecting barriers to entry, regulators and legislators have also sought to control almost every detail of an institution's operations on Indian soil. Each of the three Bills mentioned above have proposed to control the admission and fee-setting procedures of private/foreign institutions, in some cases going so far as to regulate appointments, scholarships and the distribution of seats between faculties. The Indian judiciary, normally a voice of reason on the competence of state administration, has yet to express an opinion on the issue (see Section II for the judiciary's views on private participation). The prospect seems rather bleak for foreign providers aspiring to enter the Indian market in the near future.

Current Status of Foreign Participation

The current regulatory framework has generated perverse outcomes. Because of underlying suspicions of private and foreign providers, the government puts forth complex and demanding regulations, imposing costs that legitimate foreign organisations are unwilling to bear, but that illegitimate foreign providers accept because they can recover the costs by exploiting students. Typically, these institutions make minimal capital investments in India, indeed sometimes none at all. They charge students high fees for qualifications that the institution may not be accredited to grant in its home country. Such practices only confirm the suspicions of regulators, thus perpetuating the notion that foreign providers indulge in unseemly practices. While this is true for many, the situation is actually the result of the current regulatory framework rather than the inherent quality of foreign education providers.

As of 2005, there were 131 foreign education providers in India, serving 'a few thousand' privately funded students.

Although the Government of India permits 100% Foreign Direct Investment (FDI) in higher education, foreign providers mostly tend to "twin" with an Indian institution and offer technical programmes allowing students to complete their studies in India and in the country of the foreign provider. Some also grant Indian institutions the right to deliver their courses. Fees are high in all cases. Both twinning and programme-based arrangements adopt the low-investment, high-return model of foreign involvement described earlier. This suggests the current channels open to foreign participation are less than optimal for legitimate foreign entrants and the Indian education system in general.

Increasing Dissonance in the Public Debate

One could conclude that the prospects for foreign participation in Indian higher education are extremely bleak. But in a constantly shifting landscape where divergent ideologies clash, interested foreign players can take comfort in the incoherent outlook and approach taken by Indian regulators. Despite three separate attempts, the Parliament has been unable to adopt a unified strategy towards privatisation or foreign participation in higher education. Moreover, the Indian judiciary has taken thirteen years and five judgments, yet it has not produced a clear direction on private institutions.

There is incoherence within and among the various agencies of government involved in this file. For instance, in 2005 the government was preparing a Bill to regulate private and foreign professional education providers when the Supreme Court decided (in the *Inamdar* case) to grant private colleges autonomy in admissions and fee setting, within reasonable limits. Although this led to mothballing the Bill, the political outcry against the Court's decision immediately drew a different government response. With unprecedented support from all political parties, it amended the Constitution via the Central Educational Institutions (Reservation in Admission) Act, 2006, to mandate minimum quotas for SC/

ST and Other Backward Castes (OBCs) in higher education institutions. This is a reminder that in India, it is most often politics rather than policy that gets results, in higher education as in other areas. It should come as no surprise that the current Foreign Educational Institutions Bill, due to be introduced in Parliament last year, has been withheld because members of the ruling coalition cannot reach consensus. While the parties of the Left have criticised it for not being strong enough, there have also been differences within the Cabinet between the Minister of Human Resource Development and the Minister of Commerce regarding the desirability of setting minimum quotas for minorities in foreign institutions.

The growing dissonance within government on the issue of foreign institutions is also reflected in two important policy documents—the recommendations of the National Knowledge Commission (NKC) on higher education, and the 2006 Consultation Paper on Higher Education and GATS released by the Department of Commerce (DoC). Based on the objectives of "expansion, excellence and inclusion", the NKC has, among other things, emphasised the importance of diversifying funding sources for higher education through higher user fees, efficient use of resources, and private investment. Keeping in mind the objective of quality, it has recommended that the government "formulate appropriate policies for the entry of foreign institutions into India,... while ensuring a level playing field for foreign and domestic institutions within the country."

The DoC is more encouraging about foreign participation. Given the national goals of expanding capacity and access in the system, it argues for "a mechanism whereby private and foreign investment in higher education can be encouraged subject to high quality standards and efficient regulation." This position is based on lack of public funds for India's current needs, and the economic gains of retaining at home students who can afford to pay high fees and can study abroad. The NKC's recommendations have met considerable resistance from the MHRD and UGC. Similarly, the DoC and MHRD have taken opposite sides in the debate. Needless to say, both the NKC and DoC are uniformly reviled by Left-leaning political parties, academic institutions and media.

On the surface, there appears to be growing discord over foreign presence in India's higher education sector. Indeed, this represents a welcome new phenomenon, namely public debate on the issue. The government is no longer unified behind the same anti-foreign ideology. The current debate within government and civil society indicates a new willingness to talk about foreign investment in higher education, a virtual taboo topic in India where education was considered a non-commercial enterprise of strategic importance to the country's interests and identity. For foreign institutions, governments and interest groups, this public debate presents an unprecedented opportunity to promote their cause and be heard by an increasingly attentive audience.

Opportunities and Strategies for Foreign Providers

At the outset, aspiring entrants need a reminder that there is little to be gained from a short-term perspective. The opportunities that exist within the present regulatory framework are limited, and limiting. In order to expand their scope, foreign enterprises need to engage in the long-term process of building relationships across a broad spectrum of policymakers, academics, administrators and even students. This approach underpins the following three suggested strategies.

First, foreign institutions, their representatives and other interest groups need to identify the constituencies that are sympathetic to their cause within the existing regulatory framework, be it the NKC, the DoC or any other agency. A greater level of interaction with these agencies is likely to be rewarding in the longer term. It is also important to lobby the 'establishment', *i.e.* MHRD, UGC, AICTE and other professional councils, in order to press for greater flexibility and to keep abreast of regulatory and legislative developments.

Second, foreign governments need to be convinced of the usefulness of the international trade regime as a platform for promoting foreign involvement in Indian education. Countries such as the US, the UK, Australia and Canada need to leverage their alumni networks in India, as well as their potential clientele among India's student population. While some countries have already submitted proposals in higher education under GATS, India has not made any commitments on this front. At this time, many sub-sectors within the Indian education system are not prepared for competition from international players. Therefore lobbying through the WTO is likely to take longer than any other approach.

Third, in anticipation of the Foreign Educational Institutions Bill to be enacted over the next two years, many foreign institutions have chosen to develop substantive partnerships with Indian institutions going beyond existing models of collaboration, or to prepare for involvement based on stand-alone commercial presence. It is important for such institutions to avoid the temptations of short-term gain in favour of a long-term perspective. In all likelihood, foreign actors will get the approvals they seek as India is further integrated into the global economy.

Conclusion

Foreign participation in Indian higher education hinges on the ability of the domestic regulatory system to successfully balance two conflicting objectives—building a world-class educational system, and ensuring that education remains a charitable activity that embodies national values and priorities. While the latter might seem rather anachronistic against the backdrop of the modern education system, it is nonetheless a valid concern that must be taken into account.

Fostering the 'right' kind of foreign participation will depend on understanding that the tension between these two objectives is not a zero-sum game. Regulators need to realise that it is possible to have aggregate gains that promote both objectives without giving up much beyond a degree of control over the system, which in its current state is highly controlled and inflexible. On the part of foreign institutions, it is prudent to be sensitive to local conditions and to respect domestic objectives for education. Above all, foreign actors need to accept a degree of control over their institutional autonomy in order to benefit from longer-term involvement. Lastly, it is by no means asserted here that foreign or private investment is a panacea for the ills of the current system. However, it can certainly contribute to a sector currently in dire need of improvement.

REFERENCES

1. Agarwal, Pawan. 'Higher Education in India: The Need for Change'. *ICRIER Working Paper No. 180*, June 2006.
2. Provisional estimates from University Grants Commission, *UGC Annual Report 2005-2006.*
3. UNESCO Institute for Statistics, *Global Education Digest 2007*, UNESCO, 2007.
4. *National Level Educational Statistics at a Glance (2004-05)*, MHRD; 11% from Agarwal (2006).
5. Ministry of Human Resource Development, *Selected Educational Statistics 2004-2005*, MHRD, 2007.
6. Census of India, 2001; *Population Projections for India and States 1996-2016*, Registrar General, Ministry of Home Affairs, Govt. of India; *UGC Annual Report 2005-06*, UGC, 2007.
7. Institute for Applied Manpower Research, *IAMR Manpower Profile 2005.*
8. Vijender Sharma, 'Indian Higher Education: Commodification and Foreign Direct Investment', *The Marxist*, Vol. XXIII, No. 2, April to June, 2007.
9. MHRD, *Statement indicating the Public Expenditure on Education* (www.education.nic.in/planbudget/GDP51-06.pdf) .

10. MHRD, *Analysis of Budgeted Expenditure on Education 2003-04 to 2005-06*, MHRD Dept. of Higher Education (Planning and Monitoring Unit), New Delhi, 2006.

11. Mehta, Pratap Bhanu, 'Critiquing the Regulatory Regime', *Indian Express*, 15 July, 2005.

12. Mehta, Pratap Bhanu, 'Regulating Higher Education', *Indian Express*, 14 July, 2005.

13. Kapur, Devesh and Mehta, Pratap Bhanu, 'Indian Higher Education Reform: From Half-baked Socialism to Half-baked Capitalism', *CID Working Paper No. 108*, Harvard University, Sept. 2004.

14. McBurnie, Grant and Ziguras, Christopher. 'The Regulation of Transnational Higher Education in Southeast Asia: Case Studies of Hong Kong, Malaysia and Australia', *Higher Education*, Vol.42, July 2001.

15. Mukul, Akshaya, 'UPA Claims Credit for Law Still in the Works, PMO Non-committal', *The Times of India*, May 24, 2007.

16. Dept. of Commerce, *Higher Education in India and GATS: An Opportunity*, Trade Policy Division, Department of Commerce, Government of India, 2006.

17. Trivedi, Divya, 'Foreign Educational Institutions Waiting for Foray into India', *The Hindu*, Jan 23, 2008.

18. Atlas of Student Mobility (www.atlas.iienetwork.org), A Website of the Institute of International Education; Accessed on April 10, 2008.

19. Perkins, Tara. 'Canada Tries Education in Scramble to Catch Up', *The Star*, March 08, 2007.

CHAPTER 9

Human Resource Development

—SUBHRABALA BEHERA

Introduction

Development of any sector depends upon the knowledge and skill availability. The people skill is very important aspect of food industry and its development. Like any other knowledge based industry, food industry also needs highly skilled man power of all levels to handle various operations.

Human resource is an increasingly broadening term with which an organisation or other human system describes the combination of traditionally administrative personnel functions with acquisition and application of skills, knowledge and experience. Human resources has at least two related interpretations depending on context. The original usage derives from political economy and economics where it was traditionally called labour, one of four factors of production, although this perspective is changing as a function of new and ongoing research into more strategic approaches at national levels. The first usage is used more in terms of 'Human Resource Development[HRD]' and can go beyond just organisations to the levels of nation. The more traditional usage within corporations and businesses refers to the individual within a firm or agency and to the portion of the organisation that deals with hiring, firing, training and other personal issues typically referred to as 'Human Resource Management [HRM].'

Meaning

Human resource means the education, efficiency, ability, far-sightedness productivity of the population of a country. The term Human Resource Development or Human Capital Formation means," the process of acquiring and increasing the number of persons who have the skills, education and experience which are critical for the economic and the political development of the country." Thus it is associated with investment in man and his development as a creative productive resources.

Human resource development is the framework for helping employees develop their personal and organisational skills, knowledge and abilities. Human resource development includes such opportunities as employee training, employee career development, performance management and development, coaching, succession planning, key employee identification, tuition assistance and organisation development.

The focus of all aspects of human resource development is ongoing the most superior workforce so that the organisation and individual employees can accomplish their work goals in service to customers.

Human Resource Development can be formal such as in classroom training, a college course or an organisational planning that change effort or human resource development can be informal as in employee coaching by a manager. Healthy organisations believe in human resource development and cover all of these.

Definition

The part of human resource management which specifically deals with training and development of the employees. Human resource development would include training as individual after he/she is first hired providing opportunities to learn new skills distributing resources which are beneficial for the employee's tasks and any other developmental activities.

Human resource development is in the human resource, teams and training subject. Scarcest and most crucial productive resource that creates largest and longest lasting advantage for an organisation. It resides in the knowledge, skills and motivation of people is the least mobile of the four factors of production and [under right conditions] learns and grows better with age and experience which no other resource can. 9716160590 ravi tiwari

Forms

There are many forms of development of human resources. The different forms of development of human resources are as under:

1. Education and Training
2. Health
3. Housing
4. Water supply and sanitation

Development

The objective of human resource development is to foster human resourcefulness through enlightened and cohesive policies in education, training, health, employment at levels from corporate to national (*Lawrence* 2000).

Ways of Development

Schultz observed that there are five ways of developing human resources—

(*a*) health facilities and services which include all the expenditures that effect the life expectancy, strength and stamina and the vigour the utility of people.

(*b*) on-the job training, including old type apprenticeships organised by firms.

(*c*) formally organised education at the elementary, secondary and higher levels.

(*d*) study programmes for adults that are not organised by firms including extensive programmes notably in agriculture.

(*e*) Migration of individuals and families to adjust to changing opportunities.

Thus, in organisations, in terms of sex and selection it is important to consider carrying out a thorough job analysis to determine the level of skills, technical abilities, competencies, flexibility of the employee required, etc. At this point, it is important to consider both the internal and external factors that can have an effect on the recruitment of employees. The external factors are those out with the powers of the organizations and includes issues such as current and future trends of the labour market, *e.g.,* skills, education level, government investment into industries, etc. On the other hand internal influences are easier to control, predict, and monitor, for example, styles or even the organisational culture.

Framework

Human resource development is a framework for the expansion of human capital within an organisation or (in new approaches, municipality, region or nation. Human resource development is a combination of Training and Education, in a broad context of adequate health and employment policies that ensures the continual improvement and growth of both the individual, the organisation and the national human resourcefulness. Adam Smith states, "The capacities of individuals depended on their access to education. "Kelley D., 2001, Human resource development is the medium that derives the process between training and learning in a broadly fostering environment. Human resource development is not a defined object, but a series of organised processes, with the specific learning objective. (*Nadler,* 1984), within a national context, it becomes a strategic approach to intersectional linkages between health, education and employment.

Structure

Human resource development is the structure that allows for individual development, potentially satisfying the organisations or the nation's goal. The development of the individual will benefit both individual, the organisation or the nation and its citizens. In the corporate vision, the human resource development framework views employees as an asset to the enterprise whose value will be enhanced by development.

Modern Analysis

Modern analysis emphasises that human beings are not "commodities" or "resources" but are creative and social beings in a productive enterprise. Though human resources have been part of business and organisations since the first days of agriculture, the modern concept of human resources began in reaction to the efficiency focus of Taylorism in the early 1900s. By 1920, psychologists and employment experts in the US started the human relations movement. This movement grew throughout the middle of the 20th century, placing emphasis on how leadership, cohesion, and loyalty played important roles in organisational success. Although this view was increasingly challenged by more quantitatively rigorous and loss "soft" management techniques in the 1960s and beyond, human resource development has gained a permanent role within organisations, agencies, and nations, increasingly as not only an academic discipline but as a central theme in the development policy.

Significance

Human capital plays an important role in the economic development. Recent studies made by Schultz, Harbison, and Kendrick point out that a large part of the growth of output in USA can be attributed to increased productivity which has mainly been the result of capital formation. Thus, importance of human resource development is most important and vital factor of economic development or it can be said that humans are the agents of development. Some of the importance of human resource or human capital are:

1. ***Country develops if the human resource is developed:*** To enhance economic development the state construct roads, buildings, bridges, dams, power houses, hospitals, etc. to run these units-doctors engineers, scientists, teachers are required. So if the state invests in a human resource it pays in dividend in response.
2. ***Increase in productivity:*** The better education increases skills and provision of healthy atmosphere will result in proper and most efficient use of resources (non-natural and natural) which will result in increase in economic production.
3. ***Education of socio and economic backwardness:*** Human resource development has an ample effect on the backwardness economy and society. The provision of education will increase literacy which will produce skilled human resource. Similarly provision of health facilities will result in healthy human resource which will contribute to the national economic development.
4. ***Entrepreneurship increase:*** Education, clean environment, good health, investment on the human resource will all have its positive effects. Job opportunities would be created in the country. And even business environment will flourish in the state which creates many job opportunities.
5. ***Social revolution:*** Because of human resource development, the socio-economic life of the people of a country changes drastically over all look changes, thinking phenomena changes, progressive thoughts are endorsed into the minds of people.

Problems of Human Resource Development in India

The human resource development in India faced with several problems. Important among them are :

1. ***Low priority:*** Low priority has been accorded to the development of human resources in the plans. Sectors, like agriculture, industry, transport, etc. have been given top priority.
2. ***Lack of manpower planning:*** Because of poor manpower planning, problem of employment has been mounting and human resources remain unutilised and thus are wasted.
3. ***Regional imbalances:*** There are wide differences with regard to facilities for the development of human resources in different regions of the country. The disparity between the rural and the urban areas is most marked.
4. ***Low return:*** Rate of return of investment in human resource development is generally low. Therefore, private sectors do not take much interest in its production.
5. ***Rapid growth of population:*** A poor country like India finds it difficult to spare vast resources for the development of such a large population.
6. ***Problem of Brain-drain:*** By drain-brain we mean the large scale migration of trained and skilled individuals to other developed countries. There are two serious consequences of this brain-drain- a) we spend a large amount of money on the individual's education and training; (*b*) the country is deprived of the contribution that skilled personnel could make in her economic development.

How to Develop Human Resources

1. Development of human resources shall be given highest priority by the government. The objectives of

the government shall be to adopt strategies to enable its residents to take full advantage of tremendous employment and self-employment opportunities that will be unleashed through the implementation of various economic development policies. Efforts will therefore be made to reorient education being imparted in the state with the twin objectives of meeting the requirements of enterprises from local resources and to improve the skill sets of trained manpower to improve their earning capacity.

2. To achieve these objectives, detailed schemes shall be chalked out incorporating role of industry in deciding curriculum and in management of ITI's polytechnics, and engineering colleges.
3. Special curriculum shall be evolved to produce job oriented workforce for availing opportunities in the services sector.
4. Entrepreneurship development programme should be organised to help youth set up their own ventures.
5. The role of employment exchanges shall be recast to meet the requirements of industry and in the services sector.

Ministry of Human Resource Development (MHRD)

There has been an increasing awareness that the people of the country should be looked upon as its valuable resource indeed the most valuable resource and our growth process should based on the integrated development of the citizen, beginning with childhood and going sight through life. It is increasingly realised that all relevant instruments and agencies contributing to or responsible for this growth should be integrated in order to ensure all round development. In pursuance of this area, a new ministry under a suggestive name, Ministry at Human Resource Development, on 26th Sep, 1985 through 174th Amendment Act to the Government of India (Allocation of Business) Rules 1961. Currently the ministry has two departments names:

(*a*) Department of school education and literacy.

(*b*) Department of Higher education.

Global Human Resource Development Centre [GHRDC]

The vision of setting up a "Global Human Resource Development Centre [GHRDC]" was conceived by a group of national and international management professional as early as 1997. The centre has to act as one of the key player in providing a new direction to human resource development initiatives to meet the new millennium. GHRDC has a team of professionals widely acclaimed nationally as well as internationally, representing the top leadership in the field of human resource management. Located in Delhi, GHRDC has plans to set up centers in other towns in India and abroad.

GHRDC through its centre for Management Education and Research has been engaged in—

- Research in different areas with the objective of contributing to the quality management and other professional education in the country.
- Carrying out study and survey assignments to analyse and understand the norms and expectations of national and global players in human management.
- Developing and publishing resource books and directories.
- Conduct training programmes for MBA students.
- Conduct Faculty Development programmes and MDP for B-schools.
- To support consultancy to B-schools in their capacity building through SWOT analysis, benchmarking and developing long term solutions and action plans.
- It also facilitates recruitment of directors, deans, professors, and other faculty for B-schools.

REFERENCES

1. Mclean G.N. NHRD: A Focused study in Transitioning Societies in the Developing World. In Advances in Developing Human Resources; 8, 3, 2006.
2. http//en. Wilkipedia.org/wilki/ J.E.S. Lawrence.
3. Lawrence J.E.S. Literacy and HRD: An Integrated Approach. Reprinted in Special Edition of Annals American Academy of Political and Social Science, World Literacy 2000, Vol. 520.
4. Nadler D., 2001, Dual Perceptions of HRD: Issues for policy: SME's Other Constituencies and the Contested Definitions of HRD, John Wiley and Sons, New York.
5. Kelley D., 2001 Dual Perceptions of HRD: Issues for Policy: SME's Other Constituencies and the Contested Definitions of HRD, http//ro.uow.edu.au/artspapers/26.
6. Elwood F. Holton II, James W. Trott. Jr. 1996, Trends Towards a Closer Integration of Vocational Education and HRD, *Journal of Vocational Education,*Vol. 12, No. 2, p. 7.

CHAPTER **10**

Global Meltdown and Its Impact on Indian Economy

—DR. B. ESWAR RAO PATTNAIK
DR. SUDHANSU SEKHAR NAYAK

ABSTRACT

The global economic crisis has affected Indian economy less harshly than world economies, thanks to effective management of the economy.

As credit flow dried up, there was closure of business industrial houses, loss of jobs and deferent of investment plans. The global melt down has hit hard the I.T. sector and scaled down the country's exports of textiles, carpets, leather gems and jewelleries our export market in U.S. has squeezed sizeably, while financial slow down has adversely affected inflow of remittances initially but improved in 2004-05.

Indian Cultivators

In the wake of financial liberalisation, there has been slow down in the flow of bank credit particularly commercial banks to priority sector. Bank credit flow to agriculture fell from 22.3 per cent in 2007-08 to 17.3 per cent in 2008-09, as per the economic survey 2008-09. The agrarian crisis is related to decline in the access of peasant farmers to institutional credit. In the liberalised world, peasant producers of the country had to face volatility of crop prices and volatile global environment. The impact of volatile crop prices has created compulsions on farmers to shift the cropping pattern and buy new varities of seeds supplied by MNCs. The policy initiative of the government that has reduced credit availability to farmers has created difficulties for cultivators in finding working capital for agriculture, raised input expenses and rendered farming a less viable enterprise.

It is well known that, fall in international prices of commodities like energy metals and agricultural intermediaries across the world has retarded farmers income via import competition as well low prices in sectors such as cotton and oil seeds production.

Employment Situation

It is no gain say that, in gems and jewellery, transport and automobiles, employment has declined by 8.58 per cent, 4.03 per cent and 2.43 per cent respectively. A study of 402 exporting units by survey conducted by Department of Commerce has estimated job losses to the tune of 109,513 between August 2008 to June 2009. Wage rates declined for daily wage farmers and migrant workers. Employment squeeze in organised sector gets transmitted to unorganised sector. The National Commission for enterprises in the unorganized sector floats the view that the global melt down has produced severe repercussions on unorganised poor in sectors like construction, handloom textiles, apparel, leather products, gems and jewelers, oil mills, carpets, handicrafts and marine products.

Policy Options

The government should adopt cheap money policy to inject more credit flow to develop infrastructure, real estate, corporate sector and small scale sector. There is need for providing micro credit for marginal and small farmers to protect them from the clutches of moneylenders.

There is substance in the statement that, investment may be made in projects which have short gestation period and have positive impact on output employment and income.

Till date, dependence of sizeable population on agriculture persists and industrialisation process should receive focussed attention considering backward and forward linkages of industrialisation.

Gains in growth rate of the economy are driven by performance of the service sector. Informal sector which hold the key for massive employment on the economy should receive more credit from banks.

In the era of globalisations, world economics are closely interlinked. So, the monetary and fiscal policies should be so formulated that domestic policies fit into dynamic changes of world economy. There should be programmes to boost pro-poor investment in physical and social infrastructure. To provide succour to workers in the unorganised sector social security measures like, pensions and health insurance programmes may be initiated. Programmes to protect and improve incomes of the poor is the need of the day.

Introduction

The present paper is an effort to discuss the impact of global economic crisis on Indian economy. The paper is based on secondary data assembled from research journals like: The Economist, Economic and Political Weekly, standard texts, souvenir of (62nd) All India Commerce Conference of Indian Commerce Association, Times of India and the Hindu.

Mankind has witnessed alarming financial crisis in mid 2008, in America which has taught us that the world's financial system had problems far beyond a single badly run investment bank and temporarily frozen credit markets (The Economist September 12, 2009). The five biggest investment Bank's and Lehman Brothers have vanished in the financial carnage. Wall Street and City of London have to fish in troubled waters. The biggest insurance company in the world A.I.G. was put on life support system.

Academicians endorse the view that the crisis had its roots in the recklessness of the banking system of US that had started lending money to sub-prime borrowers with no track records of loan recovery. The rationale behind such loan provision by banks to debtors was the belief that the prevailing real estate boom that had doubled home prices may persist and there by enable people with poor solvency backgrounds to redeem the loans.

The eclipse on the rosy picture was unimpeded prices (Inflation) which had created compulsions to Federal System to enhance bank rate. The net result is slowing down in real asset prices. The loans are of non-recourse loans and debtors began handing over the real estates (houses) to banks.

Impact on India

A recession can be defined as a slowing down of the activity in an economy. A decline in the GDP growth of a country over two or more consecutive quarters of a year in a country is the hallmark of recession. There is consensus that, a recession is a normal part of a business cycle and it would last between 6 months and 12 moths. Researchers state that recession is the period between when business activity after reaching a peak starts to fall and when it ultimately reaches bottom. Less spending by consumers due to lack of faith in the economy is the cardinal feature of recession. Less spending results in a decline in demand for products followed by cuts in production, rise in levels of unemployment and eventually decline in levels of GDP in a country.

(A) ***Montary Policy:*** India could not be insulated against the global turmoil uncertainty in demand projections and lack of funding for long-term capital expenditure. Fast growing sectors in India like I.T. Sector have witnessed a moderate decline the growth rate. There was a decisive squeeze on business profits which has picked up demand for upper real estate and demand for durable households declined. Amidst excess liquidity and endless inflow of foreign currency the R.B.I. has tightened the liquidity by increasing CRR or hiking repo rates or increasing risk weights to real sector to avoid real asset bubble.

Hindu editorial, observes (November 3, 2009) that the R.B.I.'s counter cyclical prudential measures, during both the credit boom and the downturn have played a significant role in minimizing the deleterious consequences of the crisis. The initiatives taken by the RBI were mainly aimed at strengthening of the banking system and financial markets, while ensuring uninterrupted flow of credit to different sectors of the economy. The monetary policy shifted its focus from monetary tightening during the first half of 2008-09 to aggressive easing in the second half using both conventional and unconventional tools. Financial innovations and invention have increased the speed and extent to which shocks are transmitted across asset classes and countries. There is a need for achieving coordination in regulatory policies across the world. In Indian context the nascent stage of development of credit derivatives market in India and perseverance policy that discourages excessive risk taking are some of the factors that helped Banks and markets insulate themselves. Understandingly, these policies have to be reviewed in order to reinforce financial stability, financial sector governance and risk management practices.

(B) *G.D.P. Growth Rate :* The global recession that has started after the recent sub-prime crisis and unprecedented rescue of several financial institutions has not affected G.D.P. growth rate of the country which is currently obtained at 6.6 per cent rate per annum. While the growth rate of agriculture has stagnated round 2 per cent per annum below the targeted rate of 4 per cent industry has registered a 7-7.2 per cent growth rate a year. of late, (from July, September 2009) period GDP has recovered to touch 7.9 per cent. The positive agricultural growth rate despite the drought, a big jump in manufacturing and a large fiscal stimulus were key drivers of growth. As observed in Decan Chronicle the corporate sector is responding, agricultural growth rate is taking place and negative growth of exports has come down in October, 2009. The I.T. sector is adversely affected due to the economy's dependence on export market.

With regard to export market of the country India has been moderately affected by global recessionary trend, as India is a domestic consumption and investment driven market where continuation of exports to growth is not much. The inflationary pressures have eased out to a comfortable level.

(C) *Direct Exposure:* MTM losses of the banking sector including private sector, due to direct exposure stood at Rs.410 crore of which, ICICI Bank alone has MTM loss of about Rs.309 crore. Besides, some state-owned banks had exposure in the instruments of these troubled US financial institutions to the tune of Rs.234 crore. Exposure of a few public sector banks to credit-linked and floating rate notes of Lehman Brothers and other troubled institutions is about USD 52 million. ICICI Bank, which has the largest exposure, has invested euro 57 million, (around $80 million) in through its UK subsidiary, ICICI Bank UK PLC, and the bank has already made a provision of about $12 million against investments in these bonds. The investment in Lehman bonds forms less than 1 per cent of the bank's UK subsidiary's assets and less than 0.1 per cent of ICICI group's total assets. Among the public sector banks, State Bank of India has an exposure of $5 million to Lehman through one of its foreign offices. Thus exposure of Indian banks and consequent losses are not very high.

(D) *The Domino Effect:* This is the major problem for India. Domino Effect explains how the losses made in bad assets affect the good assets. Suppose Lehman faces redemption and has to repay another bank it has borrowed from. If it sells the mortgage-backed bonds, whose prices have fallen, it will not raise as much as was earlier expected. So, it sells some of the other good assets or bonds which may have nothing to do with mortgages. But since the bank starts dumping these assets, prices of these bonds also dip. This is when the crisis spreads from sub-prime to prime. This led to heavy offloading of Indian stocks by these foreign investors and consequent fall of Indian capital markets.

(E) ***Indian Cultivators:*** In the wake of financial liberalisation, there has been slow down in the flow of bank credit particularly commercial banks to priority sector. Bank credit flow to agriculture fell from 22.3 per cent in 2007-08 to 17.3 per cent in 2008-09, as per the economic survey 2008-09. The agrarian crisis is related to decline in the access of peasant farmers to institutional credit. In the liberalized world, peasant producers of the country had to face volatility of crop prices and volatile global environment. The impact of volatile crop prices has created compulsions on farmers to shift the cropping pattern and buy new varities of seeds supplied by MNCs. The policy initiative of the government that has reduced credit availability to farmers has created difficulties for cultivators in finding working capital for agriculture, raised input expenses and rendered farming a less viable enterprise.

It is well known that, fall in international prices of commodities like energy metals and agricultural intermediaries across the world has retarded farmers income via import competition as well low prices in sectors such as cotton and oil seeds production.

(F) ***Employment Situation:*** It is no gain say that, in gems and jewellery, transport and automobiles, employment has declined by 8.58 per cent, 4.03 per cent and 2.43 per cent respectively. A study of 402 exporting units by survey conducted by Department of Commerce has estimated job losses to the tune of 109,513 between August 2008 to June 2009. Wage rates declined for daily wage farmers and migrant workers. Employment squeeze in organised sector gets transmitted to unorganised sector. The National Commission for enterprises in the unorganised sector floats the view that the global melt down has produced severe repercussions on unorganised poor in sectors like construction, handloom textiles, apparel, leather products, gems and jewelers, oil mills, carpets, handicrafts and marine products.

Policy Options

The government should adopt cheap money policy to inject more credit flow to develop infrastructure, real estate, corporate sector and small scale sector. There is need for providing micro credit for marginal and small farmers to protect them from the clutches of money lenders.

There is substance in the statement that, investment may be made in projects which have short gestation period and have positive impact on output employment and income.

Till date, dependence of sizeable population on agriculture persists and industrialisation process should receive focused attention considering backward and forward linkages of industrialization.

Gains in growth rate of the economy are driven by performance of the service sector. Informal sector which hold the key for massive employment on the economy should receive more credit from banks.

In the era of globalisations, world economics are closely interlinked. So, the monetary and fiscal policies should be so formulated that domestic policies fit into dynamic changes of world economy. There should be programmes to boost pro-poor investment in physical and social infrastructure. To provide succor to workers in the unorganised sector social security measures like, pensions and health insurance programmes may be initiated. Programmes to protect and improve incomes of the poor is the need of the day.

In the era of globalisations, world economics are closely interlinked. So, the monetary and fiscal policies should be so formulated that domestic policies fit into dynamic changes of world economy. There should be programmes to boost pro-poor investment in physical and social infrastructure. To provide succor to workers in the unorganized sector social security measures like, pensions and health insurance programmes may be initiated. Programmes to protect and improve incomes of the poor is the need of the day.

Conclusion

Paul Kurgman observes succinctly the damages from sustained high unemployment will last much longer. The long-term unemployed can lose their skills and even when the economy recovers they may find it hard to get a job because, they are regarded as poor risks by potential employers. It is likely that, unemployed slash their spending cash strapped state and local governments may engage in mass layoffs. Efforts may be made to offer businessmen direct incentives for employment. It's probably too late for a job-conserving programme, like the highly successful subsidy Germany offered to employers may also be encouraged to add workers as the economy expands. The Economic Policy Institute proposes a tax credit for employers who increase their pay rolls.

High unemployment does not punish today; it punishes the economy the face of a depressed economy when businesses may slash investment spending-both on plant and equipments and intangible investments in such things as product development and workers training. Spending more on recovery will lead to a stronger economy, both now and in the future and stronger economy means more a stronger government revenue. It needs reorganisation that stimulus works but we are not doing hereby enough of it.

REFERENCES

1. *The Economist,* September 12th -18th, 2009.
2. *The Hindu,* November 3, 2009.
3. *Competition Refresher,* January 2009.
4. 62nd All India Commerce Conference of Indian Commerce Association, *Souvenir,* 2009, 10-12 October, Ajmer.
5. Several Editions of *Times of India.*
6. *Competition Refresher,* November 2008.
7. Several Volumes of *Economic and Political Weekly.*
8. Paul Krugman "Obama Stimulus, Too Little of a Good Thing", *Decan Chronicle,* 3rd December, 09.
9. Paul Krugman "US Needs NREGA with a Cooler Acronym", *Decan Chronicle,* 1st December, 2009.
10. Amalesh Banerjee, India's Revival Agenda and Global Economic Crises, *Conference Volume, The Indian Economic Association,* 2009.
11. Asim K. Karmarker, Global Economic Meltdown and Its Impact on the Indian Economy, *Conference Volume, The Indian Economic Association,* 2009.

CHAPTER 11

Genesis of Global Recession and Its Impact on Indian Economy

—DR. SUDHAKAR PATRA

The global recession originated in September, 2007 with epicenter in USA is also called as global melt down or credit crunch or turmoil which has affected nations across the world in different degree. Capitalist or socialist country, developed or less developed country, all have experienced the wrath of recession. The current recession has entered in its third year and its adverse impact has reduced slowly. In economic jargon "Recession" is defined as a situation when real Gross Domestic Product (GDP) falls for two successive quarters. This recession is not as severe as a depression. In simple language, one can define a recession as a general slow down in economic activity over a sustained period of time, or a business cycle contraction. During Recession, many macro economic indicators vary in a similar way. Production as measured by Gross Domestic Product, employment, Government spending, capacity utilisation, household incomes and business profits, all fall during recession.

Historical Background

World economies have faced slow down many times. There has been recessions in the past around the globe which includes the most remembered "Great Depression". In that depression millions of people across the globe and particularly in USA lose jobs. In every decade there occurs depression. Besides current recession, there were recessions in 1980's, 1990-91, and 1996. The policy mix taken by the economists in US and Europe may be observed in such situation. There are various causes for occurrence of recession. First, tight monetary policy was implemented at the end of 1979 to fight an inflation rate and then, in 1981, expansionary fiscal policy was put in place of tone cuts and increased defence spending. In 1973, the US and rest of the world were hit by first oil shock, in which the oil exporting country more than doubled the price of oil. This held to bring inflation which was extremely unpopular. In October 1979, the Fed acted, turning monetary policy in a highly restrictive direction. The monetary squeeze was tightening in the first half of 1980, when the economy went into a mild recession. The reason for the sharp decline in the activity was tight money because inflation was still above 10 per cent and money stock was growing at only 5.1 per cent in 1981. The real money supply was falling with a policy of easy fiscal and tight monetary policies. It was found out a rise in interest rate was expected with govt. This policy of the fiscal expansion of 1984 and 1985 pushed the recovery of the economy forward.

Origin of Current Recession

The current global financial crisis is rooted in the sub-prime crisis which surfaced over two-years ago in the United States of America. During the boom years, mortgage bankers attracted by the big commissions, encouraged buyers with pour credit to accept housing mortgages with little or no down payment and without credit checks. A combination of law interest rates and large inflow of foreign funds during the booming years helped the banks to create easy credit conditions for many years. Banks lent money in the assumption that housing prices will continue to rise. Also the real estate encouraged the demand for houses as financial assets. Banks and financial institutions later repackaged these debts with other high risk debts and sold them to worldwide investors creating financial instruments called Collateralised Debt Obligations. In this way risk was passed on multifold through derivative trade.

Surplus inventory of houses and increase in interest rates led to a decline in housing prices in 2006-07 resulting in an increased defaults and foreclosure activity that collapsed the housing mutt. Consequently, a large number of properties ere up for sale affecting mortgage, investment firs and govt. sponsored enterprises which had invested heavily in sub-prime mortgages. Since the collateral debt instruments had been globally distributed, many banks and other financial institutions around the world were affected. Major banks and other financial institutions around the world have reported losses of approximately $435 billion as on 17 July, 2008. Thus with the failure of a few leading institutions in USA, the entire financial system in the world has been affected.

Causes of Global Recession

The first hint of the trouble came from the collapse of two bears Stearns hedge funds early 2007. Subsequently a number of other banks and financial institutions also began to show signs of distress. Matters really came to force with the bankruptcy of Lehman Brothers, a big investment bank, in September 2008. The reasons for the crisis are varied and complex. Some of them include boom in the housing must, speculation, high-risk mortgage loans and lending practices, inaccurate credit ratings and poor regulation.

1. Boom in the Housing Market
2. Speculation
3. High risk mortgage loan and lending practices
4. Securitisation Practices
5. Inaccurate credit ratings
6. Poor regulation

Some of the financial institution which have been the victim of crises. Lehman Brothers, American Insurance Group,

Bears Stearns, Citigroup, Bank ofAmerica, Gold Sachs, Merry Lynch, Bank of England, Satyam and Dubai World.

Impact on Indian Economy

The financial crisis erupted in a comprehensive manner in U.S. and Europe in August 2007. It was argued that India would be relatively immune to this crisis, because of the strong fundamentals of the economy and the supposedly well-regulated banking system. This argument was emphasised by the finance minister and others even when other developing countries in Asia clearly experienced significant negative impact, through transmission of study market turbulence and domestic structures. But now the crisis and entered into third year and many have termed it the worst financial crisis of the last century. The view, that the Indian economy would be less adversely affected by the global economic crisis because of limited integration and other inherent strengths has proved to be wrong. The financial melt down, morphed into a global economic downturn with the collapse of Lehman Brothers on 23 September, 2008, the impact on Indian economy was almost immediate. The economic in India that preceded the current down turn was dependent upon greater global integration in three urgency increased dependence on capital inflows, especially of the short-term variety, greater reliance on exports particularly of services, and the role played in underpinning a domestic credit-filled consumption and investment broom

Foreign Capital Flow

Capital flows could not have been an unmixed blessing for the economy as they have largely been associated with increased investment in stock market activity which in turn resulted in the build-up of inflationary pressures. As soon as the first signs of the crisis become visible in Asian, foreign institution investors (FIIs) started with drawing from the region on a noticeable scale. Credit flow suddenly tried-up reducing Indian companies access to Overseas finance but also lowering domestic liquidity and causing stock price fall and, money market interest rate spiked to above 20 per cent and remained high for the nest month. The pressure was evident in the form of lower inflows and higher outflows, yielding net outflows in the last two quarters of 2008-09. It is important to note that net capital flows declined from US $108.0 bn in 2007-08 to US $9.1 bn in 2008-09 as shown in the table below.

Table 11.1. Net capital flow to India during 2007-09

Items	Apr-March		2007-08 Jan-Mar	2008-09			
	2007 -08	2008 -09		Apr-June	July-Sept	Oct-Dec	Jan-Mar
FDI	15.4	17.5	8.5	9.0	4.9	0.4	3.2
Inward FDI	34.2	35.0	14.2	11.2	8.8	6.3	8.0
Outward FDI	18.8	17.5	5.7	2.9	3.9	5.9	4.8
FILS	20.3	-15.0	4.1	-5.2	-1.4	-5.8	-2.6
Net Capital Flow	108.0	9.1	26.0	11.1	7.6	-4.3	-5.3

Source : External Economy, 2009, RBI Publication III

Notwithstanding increased risk aversion on the part of international investors and tightness in the overseas credit markets, which affected other types of capital flows, inflows in the form of foreign direct investment (FDI) and non-resident Indian (NRI) deposits displayed resilience, reflecting continued attractiveness of India as a long-term investment destination and also the positive impact of various policy measures undertaken for improving certain types of inflows in response to the global financial crisis, FDI to India was channeled mainly into manufacturing sector (21.1 per cent) followed by financial services (19.4 per cent) and construction sector (9.9 per cent) during 2008-09.

Foreign Exchange Reserve

During 2008-09, India's foreign exchange reserves declined by US $ 58.00 down from US $ 309.7 bn as at the end of

March 2008 to US $ 251. bn on the same ate in March 2009, of this decline of US $ 58.0 bn, US $ 37.9 bn was an account of valuation changes, and the balance of US $ 20.1 bn decline reflected the financing needs of the BOP.

Table 11.2. Foreign Exchange Reserves US$Mn

End of Month	Gold	SDR	Foreign Currency Assets	Reserve Position in the IMF	Total
March 2007	6.784	2	191924	469	199179
March 2008	10039	18	299230	436	309723
March 2009	9577	1	241176	981	251735
April 2009	9231	1	241487	981	251702
May 2009	9604	1	251456	1245	262306
June 2009	9800	1	254093	12248	265142
July 2009	9800	1	255138	1248	266187

Source : External Economy, July 27, 2009, RBI Publication III

India's foreign exchange reserves, however, increased subsequently to US $ 266.2 billion by July 17, 2009, with portfolio reversing the earlier trend and turning significantly positive during 2009-10 so far. Only one of the larger banks ICICI, was partly affected but managed to prevent a crisis because of this strong balance sheet an timely action by govt., which virtually guaranteed its deposits. The equity must have seen a near 60 per cent decline in the index and wiping off of about US $ 1.3 trillion in market capitalisation since Jan, 2008, when sensex had picked up about 21,000.

Export and Import

Credit crunch tended to have a greater impact on Indian exports than imports. The difficulty of importing components or raw materials directly required for producing exportable also has a negative impact in domestic demand. Indian economy has been through the steep decline in demand for India's exports in its major markets. The impact on Indian export sectors is shown in the following table 11.3.

Table 11.3. Export, Import and balance of trade

Items		May-09	Fiscal Year		Full Fiscal Year			
			2009-10(1Q)	2008-09 (1Q)	08-09	07-08	06-07	05-06
Export	Rs. Crore	53435	107214 (17.4)	129846 (35.3)	766935 (16.9)	655863 (14.7)	571779 (25.3)	456418 (21.6)
	US$	11010	21752 (31.2)	31626 (36.5)	68707 (3.4)	163132 (29.0)	126361 (22.6)	103091 (23.4)
Import	Rs. Crore	78682	157514 (25.6)	211752 (37.8)	1305503 (29.0)	1012312 (20.4)	840506 (27.3)	660409 (31.8)
	US$	16212	31959 (38.0)	51507 (38.9)	287759 (14.3)	251654 (35.5)	185749 (27.3)	149166 (33.8)
Balance of Trade	Rs. Crore	-25247	-50300	-81906	-538568	-35644	- -268727	- -203991
	US$	-3202	-10206	-19880	-119055	-88522	-59388	-46075

Source : Current Statistics from Economic and Political Weekly,1st Aug. 2009

Information Technology

With the global financial system getting trapped in the quicksand, there is uncertainty across the Indian Software industry. The U.S. banks have huge running relations with Indian Software Companies. A rough estimate suggests that at least a minimum of 30,000 Indian jobs could be impacted immediately in the wake of happenings in the U.S. financial system. Approximately 61 per cent of the Indian IT Sector revenues are from U.S financial corporations like Goldman Sachs, Washington Mutual, Citigroup, Bank of America, Morgan Stanley and Lehman Brothers. The top five Indian players account for 46 per cent of the IT industry revenues. The revenue contribution from U.S clients is approximately 58 per cent. About 30 per cent of the industry revenues are estimated to be from financial services. The software companies may face hard days ahead.

Impact on Employment

Employment market was seriously affected by recession. The global financial crisis could increase unemployment. Layoffs and wage cuts are certain to take place in many companies where young employees are working in Business Process Outsourcing and Information Technology sectors . With job losses, the gap between the rich and the poor will be widened. It is estimated that there would be downsizing in many other fields as companies cut costs. The International Labour Organisation predicted that millions of jobs will be lost by the end of 2009 due to the crisis—mostly in "construction, real estate, financial services, and the auto sector." The Global Wage Report 2008-09 of International Labour Organisation warns that tensions are likely to intensify over the issue of wages. There would also be a significant drop in new hiring. All these will change the complexion of the job market.

Workers are low paid and as such would be prone to higher degree of social distress if rendered unemployed due to recession. It may be observed that in the manual contract category of workers, the employment has declined in all the sectors/industries. The most prominent decrease in the manual contract category has been in the automobile and transport sector where employment has declined by 12.45 per cent and 10.18 per cent respectively. The overall manual contract category of workers out to be 5.83 per cent. In the direct category of manual workers, the major employment loss is reported in the GEMS and JEWELERY (9.97%) followed by 1.33 per cent in metals. It can be known from the table 11.4. (See on next page)

Exchange Rate

Exchange rate volatility in India has increased in the year 2008-09 compared to previous years. Massive selling by Foreign Institutional Investors and conversion of their holdings from rupees to dollars for repatriation has resulted in the rupee depreciating sharply against the dollar. Between January 1 and October 16,2008, the Reserve Bank of India (RBI) reference rate for the rupee fell by nearly 25 per cent, from Rs. 39.20 per dollar to Rs.48.86. This depreciation may be good for India's exports that are adversely affected by the slowdown in global markets but it is not so good for those who have accumulated foreign exchange payment commitments.

Table 11.4. Loss in cash and job after recession

Sl. No.	Product Group	No. of Unit Survived	Loss in Export Order (in Lakhs)	Cash Loss suffered (in Lakhs)	Job loss during period
1.	Leather and Leather products	15	13762.00	1458.90	865
2.	Marine Products	6	2005.65	3457.23	220
3.	Minerals and mineral processing	5	26653.49	19.14	105
4.	Automobiles components sector	12	47910.00	7820.00	9391
5.	Coir and coir products	2	613.015	96.00	260
6.	Spices	3	2130.00	700.00	-
7.	Garment and textile	18	14228.28	2048.62	5799
8.	Handloom	4	1100.00	475.00	138
9.	Fruits, Vegetables and food items	12	2080.66	808.28	75
10.	Gems and jewelry	8	12567.41	49.93	947
11.	Handicrafts	12	3897.45	1027.30	1167
12.	Jute goods	2	534.00	150.00	300
13.	Engineering goods	6	8180.00	1521.00	140
14.	Chemicals	9	12187.14	47886.40	150
15.	Drugs and pharma	5	9160.61	1703.30	-
16.	Plastic	1	22000.00	3100.00	-
17.	Misc. product	1	200.00	200.80	10000
	Grand Total	**121**	**179210.26**	**7252.10**	**65507**

Source : Economic Survey 2008-09

Foreign Exchange Outflow

After the macro-economic reforms in 1991, the Indian economy has been increasingly integrated with the global economy. The financial institutions in India arc exposed to the world financial market. Foreign institutional investment (FII) is largely open to India's equity, debt markets and market for mutual funds. The most immediate effect of the crisis has been an outflow of foreign institutional investment from the equity market. There is a serious concern about the likely impact on the economy because of the heavy foreign exchange outflows in the wake of sustained selling by Foreign Institutional Investors in the stock markets and withdrawal of funds by others. The crisis resulted in net outflow of $ 10.1 billion from the equity and debt markets in India till 22nd Oct, 2008. There is even the prospect of emergence of deficit in the balance of payments in the near future.

Investment

The tumbling economy in the U.S is going to dampen the investment flow. It is expected that the capital inflows into the country will dry up. Investments in mega projects, which are under implementation and in the pipeline, are bound to buy more time before injecting funds into infrastructure and other ventures. The buoyancy in the economy is absent in all the sectors. Investment in tourism, hospitality and healthcare has slowed down. Fresh investment flows into India is in doubt.

Real Estate

One of the casualties of the crisis is the real estate. The crisis will hit the Indian real estate sector hard. The realty sector is witnessing a sudden slump in demand because of the global economic slowdown. The recession has forced the real estate players to curtail their expansion plans. Many on-going real estate projects are suffering due to lack of capital, both from buyers and bankers. Some realtors have already defaulted on delivery dates and commitments. The steel producers have decided to resort to production cuts following a decline in demand for the commodity.

Stock Market

The financial turmoil affected the stock markets even in India. The combination of a rapid sell off by financial institutions and the prospect of economic slowdown have pulled down the stocks and commodities market. Foreign institutional investors pulled out close to $ 11 billion from India, dragging the capital market down with it. Stock prices have fallen by 60 per cent. India's stock market index—Sensex touched above 21,000 mark in the month of January, 2008 and has plunged below 10,000 during October 2008. The movement of Sensex shows a positive and significant relation with Foreign Institutional Investment flows into the market. This also has an effect on the Primary Market. In 2007-08, the net Foreign Institutional Investment inflows into India amounted to $20.3 billion. As compared to this, they pulled out $11.1 billion during the first nine-and-a-half months of the calendar year 2008, of which $8.3 billion occurred over the first six-and-a-half months of the financial year 2008-09.

Banks

The ongoing crisis will have an adverse impact on some of the Indian banks. Some of the Indian banks have invested in derivatives which might have exposure to investment bankers in U.S.A. However, Indian banks in general, have very little exposure to the asset markets of the developed world. Effectively speaking, the Indian banks and financial institutions have not experienced the kind of losses and write-downs that banks and financial institutions in the Western world have faced .Indian banks have very few branches abroad. Our Indian banks arc slightly better protected from the financial meltdown, largely because of the greater role of the nationalised banks even today and other controls on domestic finance. Strict regulation and conservative policies adopted by the Reserve Bank of India have ensured that banks in India are relatively insulated from the travails of their western counterparts.

POLICY MEASURES

Fiscal Stimulus

The initial fiscal stimulus was actually provided in the budget for FY 2008-2009, announced in February 2008. Electoral considerations made this into an expansionary exercise that included massive increases in public outlays in support of employment guarantee schemes, farm loan waivers, pay commission rewards, and increases in food and fertilizer subsidies. This fiscal expansion is expressed by the revenue deficit increasing from 1.4 per cent of the GDP in FY 2007-2008 to 4.3 per cent in FY 2008-2009. At the same time the fiscal deficit of the Central Government increased from 2.7 per cent in FY 2007-2008 to 6.1 per cent in FY 2008-2009. The expansionary public outlays included some measures that implied a hefty transfer of purchasing power to farmers and to the rural sector in general. These included farm loan waivers, funds allocated to the National Rural Employment Guarantee Programme (NREGP), Bharat Nirman (targeted for improving rural infrastructure) Prime Minister's Rural Road Programme, and a large increase in subsidies for fertilisers and electricity supplied to the farmers.

Table 11.6. Budget Outlay on Rural Sector

(Values in US$ bn)

Sl. No	Item	FY 2008-2009 (RE)	FY 2008-2009 (BE)
1.	Bharat Nirman	6.25	8.18
2.	NREGA	6.00	6.02
3.	Fertilizer Subsidy (a) Indigenous Urea (b) Imported Urea (c) Concession Fertilizers	15.17 3.30 2.20 9.67	10.00 1.72 1.56 6.72
4.	Farm Loan Waiver	13.06	
	Total	**40.49**	**24.20**

BE = Budget Estimates, RE= Revised Estimates,
Source : Ministry of Finance, Govt. of India (2009)

These measures were taken because of political considerations and not in response to the global crisis. Nevertheless, they have helped to shore up rural demand for both consumer durables and non-durables. In effect the higher than expected GDP growth rate in both the third and fourth quarters of FY 2008-2009 could be attributed to the budgetary splurge announced in February 2008. While this has succeeded in shoring up GDP growth by raising rural demand, it did not leave much fiscal space for the Government of India to respond in any significant manner to counter the impacts of the global downturn.

Many efforts are still required to counter the effects of the global economic slow down. Three fiscal stimulus packages—one each in the months of December, January, and March—were announced. These in aggregate amounted to Rs. crore 106,050 or US$21 billion, which is approximately 2 per cent of the GDP. This can be compared to the 4 per cent of GDP that was provided as stimulus in the FY 2008-2009 budget discussed in the paragraph above. The post-December 2008 stimulus packages mainly are comprised by increased government spending on infrastructure, reduction in indirect taxes, and some assistance for export-oriented industries. In an attempt to boost the infrastructure spending that has been acknowledged as the most effective tool to counter economic downturn, the Government of India has increased its planned spending by US$4 billion and has also allowed the state governments to borrow an additional amount of US$6 billion from the market. Apart from this, the India Infrastructure Finance Company Limited (IIFCL), a special purpose vehicle (SPV) established in 2007, has been allowed to issue interest free bonds worth US$6'billion for refinancing the long-term loans for various infrastructure projects.

Secondly, to prop up domestic demand the central excise duty was gradually slashed from 14 per cent in December 2008 to 8 per cent in March 2009 on all products except petroleum products. Likewise the services tax rate has also been brought down from 12 per cent to 10 per cent. The government has also provided some relief to export-oriented industries through subsidising interest costs of exporters by up to 2 per cent, subject to a minimum rate of 7 per cent per annum. It has also allocated US$240 million for a full refund of terminal excise duty or central sales tax, wherever applicable, and another US$80 million for various export incentive schemes. The direct fiscal burden of all the aforementioned measures adds up to about 2 per cent of total GDP. This looks rather small in comparison to the size of the stimulus in some other economies like the PRC and the US. However, if we include the stimulus provided in the FY 2008-2009 budget, the Indian government has in effect expanded its fiscal outlay by 6 per cent of GDP during FY 2008-2009. It can be argued that the economy may have fared better if more fiscal space was available to boost domestic demand to counter the collapse of external demand that started in November 2008.

Monetary Policy

With the objective of maintaining price stability alongside a reasonable rate of economic growth, the last two years have been very hectic for policymakers at the RBI. After a comfortable period of low inflation, the Indian economy started feeling the pressure of rising global commodity prices in the first quarter of FY 2004-2005. In response to this rise in inflation, the RBI started tightening monetary policy in September 2004, raising the cash reserve ratios from 4.5 per cent to 5.0 per cent. As the inflationary situation worsened in the subsequent period, the tightening of monetary policy became even more aggressive. Consequently, inflation declined from around 8 per cent in the middle of 2004 to less than 4 per cent in September 2007. Nevertheless, coinciding with the rising global inflation trends, domestic inflation once again started increasing towards the end of 2007 and became a major headline in the first week of June 2008 when it entered the double-digit range for first time since the 1991 BOP crisis. It drew a sharp reaction from the RBI and the speed of monetary tightening was further increased. This credit tightening from FY 2004-2005 onward ensured a soft landing of Indian economy, which began overheating over the past three years with the actual growth rate exceeding its potential growth rate. As a result the growth rate began to slow down from the middle of FY 2007-2008.

In the wake of global financial crisis and its potential adverse effects on the Indian economy, monetary policy shifted gear and became expansionary from October 2008. The rapid decline in Wholesale Price Index inflation, which has come down from its peak level of around 13 per cent in August 2008 to less than 1 per cent in April 2009, allowed the RBI to completely shift its focus from inflation to growth. Since October 2008, the RBI has injected a considerable amount of liquidity into the economy through a series of policy rate cuts. The cash reserve ratios of banks has been brought down from 9 per cent to 5 per cent, while the REPO RATE has been slashed by 425 basis points. Further, in order to discourage the banks from parking overnight funds with the RBI, the reverse REPO RATE has been gradually reduced from 6.0 per cent in November 2008 to 3.25 per cent in April 2009. The statutory liquidity ratio (SLR) has been lowered by one percentage point(Table 11.7). Some special refinancing schemes have also been announced to improve the liquidity for certain sectors.

The cash reserve ratios reduction of 400 basis points since September 2008 alone has led to an injection of US$32.7 billion. In addition, another sum of US$12.9 billion has been injected through unwinding the market stabilisation scheme. As of April 2009, a cumulative amount of nearly US$80 billion has been pumped in to the system (RBI 2009d).As a result of the policy rate cuts, the prime lending rates of commercial banks have come down from 13.75-14.0 per cent in October 2008 to 12.0-12.5 per cent January 2009. The call money rates have also remained stable at low levels and the overnight money market rate has remained within the liquidity adjustment-facility corridor.

Table 11.7. Actual Potential Release of Primary Liquidity Since Mid-Sept, 2008

(Values in US$ bn)

1.	CRR Reduction	32.7
2.	MSS Unwinding	12.9
3.	Term Repo Facility	12.2
4.	Increase in export credit refinance	5.2
5.	Special refinance facility for SCBs (Non-RRB)	7.9
6.	Refinance Facility for SIDBI/HB/EXIM Bank	3.3
7.	Liquidity facility for MBFCs through SPV	5.1
	Total 1 to 7	**79.2**
	Memo : SLR Reduction	8.2

CRR = Cash Reserve Ratio, EXIM = Export Import, MSS=Market Stabilisation Scheme, NHB = National Housing Bank, RRB = Regional Rural Bank, SCBs = Scheduled Commercial Bank, SODBO=Small Ind. Devt. Bank of India, SLR=Statutory Liquidity Ratio, SPV = Special Purpose Vehicle.

Apart from the above-mentioned initiatives, the RBI has also liberalised the ECBs and FII related norms. To attract the foreign portfolio investors, the FII limit on corporate bonds has been increased from US$6 billion to US$15 billion. At the same time, in an attempt to boost the construction sector, developers have been permitted to raise ECBs for integrated townships projects, while NBFCs dealing exclusively with infrastructure financing have also been allowed to access ECBs from multilateral or bilateral financial institutions.

It could be argued that the three fiscal stimulus packages, in conjunction with the transfer of purchasing power to the rural economy through increased budget outlays on the rural sector and the hike in minimum support prices of various crops, have saved aggregate demand and prevented GDP growth from plummeting in to negative territory. This has also been helped by the quick monetary policy response discussed above. Our shock-augmented leading indicator model that some experts at ICRHER have been using to forecast GDP growth for India" verifies this hypothesis. With the full impact of the external shock, we were expecting a growth rate of 5.3 per cent in the fourth quarter of FY 2008-2009. Nevertheless, with an actual growth rate of 5.8 per cent, our calculation suggests that the fiscal stimulus has neutralised nearly 20 per cent of the impact of the external shock. If we go with this line of argument, it seems that the growth will pickup marginally in the coming quarters because the monetary policy measures taken so far are expected to come in to play. Despite this, any hope for a major revival of economic growth in FY 2009-2010 looks unrealistic as the positive impact of fiscal measures, such as the implementation of 6th Pay Commission, is bound to taper off, According to our revised forecast, in a best-case scenario GDP would grow by 6.0 per cent in FY 2009-200 while in the worst-case scenario it would only manage a growth rate of 5.0 per cent. Other agencies like the IMF, World Bank, and? ADB have also estimated Indian GDP growth in FY 2009-2010 at similar levels in their latest forecasts released in March 2009. Thus, the Indian economy will come down from the 9.0 per cent level that it had achieved in the last four years to 6.0-6.5 per cent. The growth targets for the XI Plan will also have to be lowered.

Policy Suggestions

Policy package to mitigate adverse effects of recession include the following specific measures:

1. Any further monetary policy easing or fiscal stimulus runs the grave danger of laying the foundation for a future high inflation phase. Give the long lags in monetary and fiscal policy (between two to three quarters), the effects of the policy measures taken so far are likely to take effect towards end-2009, just about the time when the excess capacity in the economy is estimated to be working it self out.

2. There is no denying that the failure of credit delivery to micro small and medium enterprises (MSMES) is having systemically important effects in spreading the recessionary virus and in aggravating social distress due to job losses. It is not time to strike out boldly by attempting measures like government guarantees of loans to MSMES on the lines of the Mandelson Plan in the UK. Actually there is provision for credit guarantees under the Deposit Insurance and Credit Guarantee Corporation (DICGC) Act 1961. However this has now become defunct. The DICGC Act 1961. However this has no become defunct. The DICGC needs to be strengthened with an infusion of funds and entrusted with the responsibility of administering such a scheme.
3. As a purely temporary measure, for the duration of the crisis, loans above a certain limit to industries in sensitive sectors can be tied to some employment protection guarantees.
4. Encouraging the adoption of innovative schemes like SMECARE and SMEHELP by other banks on an extensive scale.
5. Financial crises affect vulnerable sections of society far more than on-vulnerable sections. Hence in the interests of such sections, ensuring against financial contagion should receive top priority.

Conclusion

The Indian Economy is being affected by the spill-over effects of the global financial crisis. Great savings habit among people, strong fundamentals, strong conservative and regulatory regime have saved Indian economy from going out of gear, though significant parts of the economy have slowed down and there is a wide variance of opinion about how long it will continue. Besides this Enhanced allocation of resources for national flagship schemes such as National

Rural Employment Guarantee Scheme(NREGS) (rise by 144 per cent), Bharat Nirman (rise by 45 per cent), National Highway Development Programme (rise by 23 per cent), Jawaharlal Nehru Urban Renewal Mission(JNNURM) (rise by 87 per cent), the general election 2009 and the sixth pay commission hike in salary etc. have insulated India from the global shocks. It is expected that growth will be moderate in India. The most important lesson that we must learn from the crisis is that India must be self-reliant. Though World Trade Organisation (WTO) propagates free trade, we must adopt protectionist measures in certain sectors of the economy so that recession in any part of the globe does not affect our country.

REFERENCES

1. *Economic and Political Weakly,* March 28, 2009.
2. *Economic* Survey, 2008-09.
3. *The Hindu*, Daily, November 26, 2008, (p. 14) October10, 2008 (p. 11).
4. RBI (2009) : *"Third Quarter Review,* January, 2009".
5. *Dharitri, Oriya Daily,* 25 October, 2008 (p. 4).
6. Atreya Manahar M (2008). The US Financial Crisis : Impact on Indian IT Sector. From http://www.vcicle.com.
7. Chandrasekhar CP, Ghosh Jayati,(2008): Indian and Global Financial Crisis : from http://www.macroscan.org.
8. Chidambaram P (2008) Spill–Over effects of global crisis will be tackled. *The Hindu, Daily,* November, 19 2008 (p. 15).

CHAPTER **12**

Global Recession and Its Impact on Indian Economy

—PRABIN KUMAR PADHY

Introduction

On 15th September 2008 the global economy contemplated the worst financial turmoil since the Great Depression of 1930 being triggered by the idiosyncratic spurt in mortgage delinquencies and foreclosures in the United States with adverse consequences for banks, financial markets, exports, employment, wages and salaries, consumer expenditure and tax revenue collections all over the world. The sprawling financial contagion across the globe was marked by the debacle of the major US Investment Bank, Lehman Brothers, The genesis of the crisis can be traced back to the recklessness or financial profligacy of the US Banking system that disbursed loans to sub-prime borrowers who had no track record of redemption of loans from their income. Sub Prime lending was advanced with speculative bubbles or with the extrapolation that the real estate boom would enable the debtors even with dodgy credit backgrounds to reimburse the loans as domestic prices escalate at an unprecedented rate. The global financial crisis germinating from 15th September 2008 not only shattered US economy but the global economy was entrapped in the Cobweb of depression. The crisis originated when Lehman Brothers the fourth largest US Securities House established in 1850 plunged into bankruptcy protection in New York when it failed to survive the global financial turmoil and lost colossal amount of $ 639 billion. Its rival Morgan Stanley was purchased by Bank of America at half of the prevailing market capitalisation price to save the ailing company. The World's biggest insurance company American Investors Group(AIG) sought financial assistance of $ 85.

The countries those have deeper economic relationship with advanced countries particularly USA, are affected more than those who maintained a closed economic status. Continentwise Europe is more affected than the countries of Asia. In Asia, China, Japan and East Asian countries are relatively more affected than the other Asian countries. The GDP growth rate in Japan has reached the lowest level of about zero per cent. The economies of Germany, France and China have been facing severe recession. On 26th January 2009 about 80,000 employees lost their jobs in US and EU. In January 2009, about 20 lakhs employees were retrenched in US and EU. In 2008, about 26 lakhs employees lost their jobs in US and EU. International Labour Organisation's Global employment trend report-2009 has said that global unemployment in 2009 could increase over 2007 by a range of 18 million to 30 million workers and more than 50 million if the economic situation continues to deteriorate in developing countries.

Objectives of the Study

The important objectives of the present study are as follows:

1. To study the concept of recession or economic slow down.
2. To examine nature, and extent of recession/economic slowdown on India
3. To assess impact of recession on Indian Economy
4. To derive implications of global recessions for an Indian Economy

Hypothesis of the Study

A hypothesis of the present research study is mentioned below:

> "India is not away from the phenomenon of global recession. But Indian Economy has been considerably affected by the global slow down.

Data and Methodology Applied

For this study a period of five years have been selected, starting from 2004-05 to 2008-09. The study relies on the secondary data published by the Government of India, RBI, IMF, CSO and others such as Economic Survey, Annual Report and others. The present study makes use of the parameters like GDP, Growth in Foreign Trade, Foreign Direct Investment, Inflation, and Employment. The entire study is based on Secondary data and information elicited from EPW competition, Refresher Publications, Standard Books, Economic Times, Times of India newspapers and Economic Survey of Government of India, Websites of Ministry of Commerce, Ministry of Finance, Ministry of Labour and Reserve Bank of India.

Occurrence of Global Financial Crisis

A global financial crisis is a reality and impacted all countries linked with world trade. It has not occurred all of a sudden in one throw, but slowly developed into a crisis affecting governments all over the world. The seeds of the crisis were sown in good times (post 9/11 recession of 2001) with a large monetary policy and free macroeconomic environment. The world continues to discuss about the role of six suspects—Alan Greenspan, Bill Clinton, George Bush, The Banks, The System of fair value accounting and the credit rating agencies. Here we will discuss the role of six issues which played major role in bringing the financial crisis in the U.S. economy.

1. Alan Green Span: It is said that the former chairman of U.S Federal Reserve Bank played an important role in the financial crisis. The monetary policy of low rate of interest was initiated. An enormous amount of liquidity was pumped into the global monetary system during 2001-05 with the short term interest rates reduced to 0.1 per cent (their lowest ever in 50 years). In order to deal with the economic slowdown following the stock market crash, the Federal Reserve has driven the cost of capital significantly below the natural rate over four years. The artificially low interest rates made excessive risk taking possible lending to the subprime crisis. It was only in his 24th October 2008 testimony to the US Congress Greenspan said, he made a mistake in the hands of regulatory philosophy.

2. Bill Clinton: President Bill Clinton is also responsible for this financial crisis. It looks that President Bill Clinton wanted in this way. In 1994 President Bill Clinton directed U.S department of Housing and Urban development to follow the plan of cheap housing loan for people. The housing loan disbursements deviated from the commercial considerations. President Clinton extensively promoted the social cause of wider home owning. With incentive for aggressive loan disbursements banks poured billions of dollars of loans with incomplete documentation.

3. George Bush Regime: The scenario did not change much during eight years of the George Bush regime. The use of sub prime mortgages continued. The share of Mortgage organisations that were sub prime increased from 5 per cent in 2001 to more than 20 per cent in 2006. U.S. house owners enjoyed an average increase of more than 54 per cent in the value of their houses. The Bush administration could not recognise these facts. Bush administration missed the presence of a bubble in the U.S. housing market and as long as home prices were rising. When the lower middle class people (borrowers) could not repay, the unprecedented financial crisis erupted. When the borrowers were not able to pay, it was the duty of bank inspector to catch the failure. These loans turned into bad loans translated into a global misfortune.

4. Government Sponsored Enterprises(GSES) and the Investment Bankers: Although U.S. does not have preferred lending rates for small housing, it has the government sponsored enterprises (GSES) created by the U.S. Although some private Companies Fannie and Freddie are working as Government Sponsored Enterprises established by the Federal Law, they received special privileges. The most important of these privileges is the notion of an implicit guarantee, so that the investors tend to believe that if these Government Sponsored Enterprises are threatened with failure, the federal government will come to their rescue. But it did not happen because the extent of leveraging and innovative derivative investments played important roles in this regard. It has been seen that while commercial banks cannot leverage their equity more than 15 to 1, but Lehman Brothers had a leverage of more than 30 to 1 and with such a high leverage, a mere 3.3 per cent drop in the value of assets could wipeout the entire value of equity and made the company insolvent. So high leverage, the lack of proper work, absence of transparency, all made these transactions led to country's economy into serious recession.

5. The system of Fair Value Accounting: The Fair Value Accounting system also failed to check the accounting system in the U.S. economy and this has led the economy into recession. Under this Accounting System (FVA) companies are required to measure financial investments at estimates of their prices they would receive if they were to sell the assets or would pay if they were to be relieved of the liabilities. So, under FVA , companies report losses when the fair value of their assets decrease or liabilities increase. Although fair values have played a role in US, financial institutions suffered huge losses on account of valuation. Lehman Brothers accepted this blunder mistake that they suffered losses of 7 billion on residential and commercial mortgages leading to company's downfall.

6. The Credit Rating Agencies: As many of the structured products like MBS or CDOs don't have a market and their valuation depended heavily on the rating agencies. In 2007, the Securities and Exchange Commission initiated examinations of three major rating agencies to review their role in bringing recession in the economy. The Commission found that there was a substantial increase in the number of and the complexity of deals related to structured products since 2002, and some of the rating agencies have struggled with the growth. The significant aspects of the rating process were not always disclosed, the rating agencies did not always document significant steps in the rating process.

Contrary to the popular perception, the real estate crisis is only a symptom of the larger financial crisis. The real estate crisis is rooted in the strategy of financial capital to bring in ever more liquidity into lending and speculation. While the massive transfer of investment capital from federal treasury to mortgage backed securities played an important role in extending the crisis to the housing sector at the expense of turning the real estate into unreal estate. And, hence the crisis was precipitated.

The causes of the Financial crisis include mortgage repayment defaults, high risk lending, excessive speculation during boom period, high personal and corporate debt level, large scale sale of risky securities on the support of dubious credit ratings, Lack of proper financial regulations in US and European Countries and the international trade imbalances and lack of proper Government regulations.

LOAN DEFAULTS AND GLOBAL FINANCIAL CRISIS

A default loan taken by lower middle class family in mid-west America led to the unprecedented global financial tsunami. If a borrower is unable to repay a loan taken from the bank, than the bank has to provide for this loan default, if a bank fails, it is the duty of the bank inspector to identify this failure and set right. Both the Bank and the inspector were lax in their duties. Further, all the loans taken from the banks scripted the same story. Hence the failures of default loans turned into a global misfortune.

How to Predict a Recession

Although there are no completely reliable predictors, the following are regarded to be possible predictors. Normally a significant stock market drop, Inverted Yield Curve, the model developed by Economist Jonathan H Wright, using a 10 year and three month Treasury Securities as well as the Fed's overnight funds rate, the three month change in the unemployment rate and initial jobless claims.

Analysis of the Crisis and Views of the Economists

The fundamentalists argue that recession takes place due to the technological shocks. Real Business cycle theory, the hard core fundamentalist find explanation of downturn in capital recession and prescribe in Walrasian from work, that the recession will pass through the natural process of creative destruction and then the equilibrium will be restored. They consider the recession as a necessary remedial process of the capitalist economy which is prone, to short run and long run fluctuations. Real business cycle theories point out the output fluctuations results from changes in technology which brings about changes in production function from period to period.

At the time of Great Depression of 1930's the classical solutions failed to pull the global economy out of depression. At that time Keynes came forward for the rescue of the world economic system. Keynes showed the inability of the "classical laissez failure "to maintain continuous, sufficient, total demand and production and employment or its liability to fall at intervals into depression and unemployment. Keynes explained the trade cycle as occurring due to fluctuations in propensity to consume, liquidity preference and marginal efficiency of capital is affected by future yield of capital goods. These expectations are subject to sudden changes. The classical prescription of increasing the money supply failed to save the world economy because the new money created went just to satisfy the increased liquidity. Thus Keynes abandoned the hypothesis of self correcting market forces and instead argued to enhance the level of government spending. He showed the way out of the depression through government intervention. Keynes was a supporter of active macroeconomic policy, involving intervention of Government, in contrast to the free play of market forces as advocated by the classical economists. Keyness influenced the macroeconomic policy after 1930 in a large way. But, in the decade of 1970's doubts were raised against Keynesian economics. Mckinnon's hypothesis which condemned the intervention of the government in the financial sector supported the idea of deregulation.With the fall of Berlin Wall and disintegration of the Soviet Union, popularised as the "End History" by Francis Fukuyama, the world once again moved towards free market fundamentalism and laissez faire ideology of the classical. The idea of Keyness were sidelined in the over optimism that the market is most efficient, and the result was worldwide recession.

The depression period was divided into three phases(1) Otober 1929 to June 1930 (2) The fourteenth month period from July 1930 to August 1931 and the third period (3) covering sixteenth month from September 1931 to December 1932. During the first phase primary producing countries were affected, with filthy exports and export prices and consequent balance of payment difficulties. During the second phase depression spread to manufacturing countries and affected employment, income prices, stock markets, government budgets, and balance of payment. During this phase Britain and some other countries suspended gold standard. During the third phase depression depended monetary measures were found wanting. Banking crisis were in many countries including India. Depression in Indian Economy resulted in rise of overdues of loans of agricultural cooperative, societies, fall of railway freight, fall of coal and cotton production. By second half of 1930, output of Jute, cotton, paper, cement, iron, and steel made some progress. Rooservelt came to office in March 1933 and came out with New Deal which suspended gold payments by banks and by implication gold standard. Direction action came in effect through National Recovery Act in USA.

Reputed Economists Nobel laureate like Joseph Stiglitz and Prof. Paul Krugman Nobel Laureate in 2008 strongly argued that the collapse was inevitable based on the size of the financial bubble. Positive public intervention became inevitable to rescue the world economy and Dr. J. Stiglitz is correct when he observed that no one can afford to not be Keynision as until 2007 (before crisis zoomed) no one can afford to be called to be a Keynesian. According to Prof. Krugmen the Nobel Laureate, the prospects for fundamental financial reform in USA are fading. The USA banking crisis is not over. The period of economic weakness is likely to continue and the real recovery of the economy be postponed.

GLOBAL IMPACT: ON WESTERN DEVELOPED COUNTRIES

The Wall street collapse of 1929 rapidly grew into Great Depression which heavily crippled the US economy, the United Kingdom(U.K.) and Western Europe. By 1933, the macro unemployment rate in US had reached to nearly 25 per cent, its manufacturing output fell to 54 per cent (of its 1929 level). The UK and German Economics, being closely linked with US economy have been severely hit. World receives everyday adverse economic news. The US Budget deficit in 2009 the largest so far is likely to reach $1.9 trillion, compared to $ 1 trillion in 2008. Toyota, big automobile corporation, announced, its first ever losses. The once popular housing Mortgage companies, Freddie Mac and Fannie Mac, the biggest insurance company, AIG and largest banks like City Bank survive on Government dollars pumped in by US Government. The largest automobile company of the world, General Motors Corporation became bankrupt. US Government extended financial help of $19.4 billion to lift the company from morass. Immediately, General Motors will have access to $15 billion in government funds. The US Government will extend federal help of another $30billion to fund its operations. General Motors shed its Pontiac, Saturn, Hummer, and Saab brand and cut loose more than 2,000 of its 6.ooo dealerships. It could result more than 1,00,000 additional job losses, General Motors along with dozen other companies became bankrupt, were :

1. Washington Mutual
2. Refco Inc
3. Delta Airlines
4. Conseco Inc
5. UAL Corporation
6. Worldcorn Inc
7. Global Crossing Limited
8. Enron Corporation
9. Pacific Gas & Electric Company
10. General Motors Limited
11. Lehman Brothers
12. Freddie Mac
13. Fannie Mac

During the last quarter, of 2008, the US economy fell by 6 per cent per year. Euro Zone declined by 1.5 per cent, Japan fell by a high level of 12.1 per cent per year. Britain, Russia, and Canada experienced recession, while Chinese, Brazilian, and South Korean and Indian Economies fell down rapidly. Smaller economies such as Spain, Mexico, Ireland, Singapore, Greece, Hungary, Pakistan and Ukraine are in dire straits. The adverse situation is faced by these economies despite a massive bail out package by governments. For example USA has give higher package of $88 trillion and spent $2 trillion in 2009. Such bailouts aggregate to more than $ 11trillion.

USA followed a model of leveraged investment, credit consumption, finance and growth. The financial crisis in US revealed the collapse of this model as it is linked with the unregulated derivatives market. In fact USA used world savings (due to supremacy of its dollar) particularly that of China as it implemented a model of high savings, over investment in USA to help it achieve export growth. Not only both the models failed , but it led to the global economic crisis. The two giants USA, China are responsible for more than half of the World's economic growth during six years (2002 to 2008). One half did the savings (China) and the other half did the spending (USA) as China's international reserves (estimated at $ 2trillion) helped to finance US current account deficit and also allowed China's exports feasible. In other words USA total debts (in 2008) exceeded the sum of their debts in the previous 40 years. USA savings fell from 5 per cent to less than zero per cent of gross national income and that of China rose from 30 per cent to 45 per cent. This relationship also extended to rest of Asia(export driven) which increased trade deficits and have house hold indebtedness in USA and also spread to Europe. The crisis was rapidly creeping up willingly supported by government deregulation and loose liberalism which forced them to offer substantial bail out programme with strong fiscal implications. The crisis led to exceptional bail out plans in US and Europe, such assistance represented 12 per cent of GDP of USA, 8 per cent in U.K. during 2009. Studying July 2, 2009 Thursday, Jobs report, Nobel Laureate in Economics in 2008 pointed out to US President Barack Obama that Since, the global recession began the USA economy has lost 6.5 million jobs. The United States has to create 1,00,000 plus new jobs each month to keep pace with the growing population and new job entrants entering into the market. On the whole, the US economy needs to create 8.5 million Jobs to fill up the gap created in the economy. IMF's estimates of growth in world output indicate that the slowdown is severe and widespread. The estimates are as following are as shown in the following table.

Table 12.1

	2007	2008	2009	2010
World Output	5.1	3.1	-1.4	2.5
Advanced Economies	2.7	0.8	-3.8	0.6
United States	2.0	1.1	-2.6	0.8
Euro Area	2.7	0.8	-4.8	-0.3
Germany	2.5	1.3	-6.2	-0.6
France	2.3	0.3	-3.0	0.4
Italy	1.6	-1.0	-5.1	-0.1
Spain	3.7	1.2	-4.0	-0.1
Japan	2.3	-0.7	-6.0	1.7
United Kingdom	2.6	0.7	-4.2	0.2
Canada	2.5	0.4	-2.3	1.6
Other Advanced Economies	4.7	1.6	-3.9	1.0
Newly Industrialised Asian Economies	5.7	1.5	-5.2	1.4
Emerging and Developing Economies	8.3	6.0	1.5	4.7
Africa	6.2	5.2	1.8	4.1
Sub-Sahara	6.9	5.5	1.5	4.1
Central and Eastern Europe	5.4	3.0	-5.0	1.0
CIS	8.6	5.5	-5.8	2.0
Russia	8.1	5.6	-6.5	1.0
Developing Asia	10.6	7.6	5.5	7.0
China	13.0	9.0	7.5	8.5
India	9.4	7.3	5.4	6.5
Brazil	5.7	5.1	-1.3	2.5
Mexico	3.3	1.3	-7.3	3.0

Source: IMF, The figures of 2009 and 2010 are projections

IMPACT OF GLOBAL RECESSION ON THE INDIAN ECONOMY

Initial impact of financial meltdown in US economy was rather muted. The reduction in the US Fed Funds rate in August 2007, in the wake of sub-prime crisis, resulted into massive increase in net capital inflow into India. The Reserve Bank of India had to sterilise the liquidity impact of large foreign exchange purchases through a series of increases in the cash reserve ratio, from 6.00 per cent on March 3, 2007 to 9.00 per cent on August 30, 2008, and issuance under the market sterilisation scheme. Thus, direct effect of the sub-prime crisis on Indian Banks/financial sector was almost negligible, because the Indian Banking System had no direct exposure to the sub-prime assets or failed institutions. It has very limited off-balance sheet activities as securitised assets. Indian Banks continue to remain sound and healthy. Secondly, Indian financial sector's limited exposure to complex derivatives and other prudential policies put in place by the Reserve Bank, kept the system rather unaffected. Thirdly, the relatively lower presence of foreign banks in India

Table 12.2

Month	Foreign direct investment	Portfolio investment	Total Inflow
April 2007	1643	1974	3617
May 2007	2120	1852	3972
June 2007	1298	3664	4962
July 2007	705	6713	7418
August 2007	831	(-)2875	(-)2048
September 2007	713	7081	7794
October 2007	2027	9564	11591
November 2007	1864	(-)107	1757
December 2007	1558	5294	6852

(Contd...)

Month		Foreign direct investment	Portfolio investment	Total Inflow
January	2008	1767	6739	8506
February	2008	8670	(-)8904	(-)234
March	2008	4438	(-)1600	2838
	2007-08	34362	29395	63757
April	2008	3740	(-)880	2860
May	2008	3932	(-)288	3644
June	2008	2392	(-)3010	(-)618
July	2008	2247	(-)492	1755
August	2008	2328	593	2921
September	2008	2562	(-)1403	1159
October	2008	1497	(-)5243	(-)3746
November	2008	1083	(-)574	509
December	2008	1362	30	1392
January	2009	2733	(-)614	2119
February	2009	1488	(-)1085	403
March	2009	1956	(-)889	1067
	2008-09	35168	(-)13855	21313

Source: Monthly Bulletin, Reserve Bank of India April 2009,Sept-2009

Banking sector also minimised the direct impact on the domestic economy. However, following a failure of investment banks in US, there was panic in capital markets in India. There was a net outflow of US $ 1403 million in September 2008 and US $5243 million in October 2008. Outflow of capital continued in November 2008, January, February, March 2009 respectively. It caused pressure in foreign exchange market. The foreign direct investment decreased from US $ 1497 million in October 2008, US $ 1083 million in November 2008 and US $ 1362 million in December 2008 from US $ 3932 million in May 2008.

Impact on Capital Market

Indian Capital Market crashed form the high of 21,000 in January 2008 to a low of 8,500.54 in October 2008. After recording strong growth during 2006 and 2007, the primary capital market received a jerk in 2008. Total amount of capital raised through equity shares during 2008 was 49,485 Crores, recording a decline of 15.7 per cent as compared to the level of 2007. The total number of Initial Public Offerings was only 37 in 2008 as compared to 100 in 2007. The amount mobilised by Initial Public Offerings in 2008 was Rs. 18,393 Crores which was lower by 45.8 per cent as compared to 2007. The net outflow of savings into Mutual Funds, which had recorded a steady rise during 2007-08, turned negative in 2008 and recorded a net outflow of Rs. 12506 Crores.

Impact on Foreign Trade

India's exports growth turned negative in October 2008, when exports contracted by 15 per cent on a year to year basis with the US and EU already fell down into recession. India's exports declined a record of 33.3 per cent in March 2009, as the continued global economic recession affected demand for goods shipped from Indian. Advanced countries like US, and Europe which account for more than 35 per cent of India's exports are experiencing a slump in demand. Imports declined by 34 per cent to $ 15.6 billion in the month under consideration in part due to the fall in commodity prices. Export growth declined from 26.7 per cent in 2007-08 to 3.4 per cent in 2008-09, had a direct bearing on GDP growth rate which declined to 6.7 per cent in 2008 09 from 9.0 per cent in 2007-08

Impact on the Real Economy

The industrial production declined to 2.8 per cent in 2008-09 from 8.8 per cent in 2007-08. The service sector growth was 9.7 per cent in 2008-09, compared to 10.5 per cent in 2007-08.The GDP growth rate was 6.7 per cent in 2008-09, as compared to 9 per cent in 2007-08. On the expenditure side, growth of private final consumption expenditure decreased to 6.6 per cent in 2008-09 compared to 8.3 per cent in 2007-08.India's industrial output declined by 1.2 per cent in February 2009 as against 9.5 per cent growth.

The growth scenario of Indian economy changed during 2008-09, under the black shadow of global recession. Higher growth rate registered during 2005-06(9.5%), 2006-07(9.7%), 2007-08(9.0%), declined to 6.7 per cent in 2008-09.

Table 12.3

Sl. No.	Sector	2003-04	2004-05	2005-06	2006-07	2007-08	2008-09
1.	Agriculture, Forestry, and fishing	10.0	0.0	5.8	4.0	4.9	1.6
2.	Mining andquarrying	3.1	8.2	4.9	8.8	3.3	3.6
3.	Manufacturing	6.6	8.7	9.1	11.8	8.2	2.4
4.	Electricity, gas & water supply	4.8	7.9	5.1	5.3	5.3	3.4
5.	Constructions	12.0	16.1	16.2	11.8	10.1	7.2
6.	Trade, hotels, and restaurants	10.1	7.7	10.3	10.4	10.1	9.0
7.	Transport, storage and communication	15.3	15.6	14.9	16.3	15.5	9.0
8.	Financing, insurance, real estate, business services	5.6	8.7	11.4	13.8	11.7	7.8
9	Community, social and personal services	5.4	6.8	7.1	5.7	6.8	13.1
	Total GDP at Factor cost	8.5	7.5	9.5	9.7	9.0	6.7

Source: Central Statistical Organisation

India as an emerging market suffered heavily than it was planned. The impact has been quite heavy. According to Reserve Bank of India Governor, D. Subba Rao, it occurs through three channels as trade channel, the financial channel, and confidence channel. Through, trade channel, it was found to be bearable as it would affect growth only by 1 to 1.5 per cent (because Merchandise exports may form about less than 15 per cent of GDP). But through financial Channel, the situation different, it is seen by financial integration which would be the ratio of total external transactions (gross current account flow plus gross capital flows). This ratio has doubled from 46.8 per cent in 1997-98 to 117.4 per cent in 2008. When such integration takes place, impact occurs in three related ways: reducing Indian companies access to overseas finance, lowering domestic liquidity, and causing stock prices to fall.

Due to global conditions Indian firms access to global finance was very much limited in various forms. Fresh external commercial borrowings have become difficult and existing ones are not easily paid. One can see the higher impact on the Indian economy. We can imagine the higher impact on the Indian Economy from foreign flows-Foreign direct investment and foreign institutional investors. The gap between domestic investment and savings (called current account deficit)of nearly 1.5 per cent of GDP reveals the potential impact on the Indian economy of foreign inflows. If the current account deficit is of 1.5 per cent, the economic growth should not decline by 0.5 to 1 per cent. But in real practice, the GDP has fallen by 2.3 per cent from 2007-08 to2008-09, the projection for 2009-10 is around 6 per cent. Which means financial integration has taken place. In 2009 the adverse balance of payments position reduced the reserves to $2.5 billion (from April-Sept. 2009) from $ 40.4 billion (April-Sept 2008) which affected domestic liquidity. Foreign Institutional Investors Inflows in April-September 2008 09) were $ 6.6 billion, compared to $ 15.5 billion in 2007-08.

Indian Banks were less affected by the global financial crisis, in the banking system of US and Europe. In India,

Banks were restrained and constrained by Reserve Bank of India by its vigil monitoring eyes. Through different channels banks got affected from the slowing down of the economy. But our country is less impacted to the global financial crisis compared to USA, Europe, Japan and other developed countries. The top persons of our Indian Economy Reserve Bank of India, Governor Dr. D. Subba Rao, and Economist and top political administrator of our country Dr. Manmohan Singh have taken the correct policy decision of the Government of India

Monetary Measures taken by the Government of India and the RBI

To lift the economy out of the recession, the Indian Government announced a fiscal and monetary package of Rs. 35,000 Crores, on December 7, 2008, which constituted 0.6 per cent of GDP. The major steps in terms of stimulus package announced by the Government of India were in the following areas:

*1. **Housing:*** A refinance facility of 4,000 Crores was provided to the National Housing Bank and all the public sector banks announced loans to needy persons at the reduced rates. It will give fillip to other sectors such as steel, cement, brick kilns. Besides the small and medium industries would get an impetus by manufacturing all kinds of fittings and furnishing. The loans were extended in order to boost the retailing sector.

(*a*) Loans upto Rs. 5 Lakhs, Maximum interest fixed at 8.5 per cent.

(*b*) Loans from Rs. (5-20) Lakhs , Maximum interest rate at 9.25 per cent.

(*c*) No processing charges to be levied from the borrowers

(*d*) No penalty is to charged in case of pre-payment.

(*e*) Free life insurance cover for the entire outstanding amount.

(*f*) The borrower can get a loan of 90 per cent of the value of the house.

2. Textiles: The textiles sector has been seriously affected due to the declining orders from the world's largest market the United States. An allocation of Rs. 1400 Crores has been made to clear the entire backlog in the Technology Upgradation Fund (TUF) scheme.

3. Infrastructure: To boost the infrastructure, the India Infrastructure Finance Company Ltd(IIFCL) has been authorised to raise 14,000 Crores through tax free bonds which will be used to finance infrastructure, especially highways and ports.

4. Exports: The Government of India has provided Rs. 1450 Crores to export sector. The government has withdrawn export duty on iron ore fines. The levy on export of lumps has been reduced to 5 per cent from 15 per cent. Exports which accounted for 22 per cent of the GDP are expected to fall by 12 per cent. The government' s fiscal package provides a interest subsidy of 2 per cent on exports for the labour intensive sectors such as textiles, handicrafts, leather, gems and jewellery.

5. Small and Medium Enterprises: The Reserve Bank of India is providing Rs. 7000 Crores to Small Industries Development Bank of India(SIDBI) for direct lending to employment of intensive micro and small enterprises (MSE). There is a reduction of 4 per cent in excise duty on cars, steel, cement, and a host of other products. The ad valorem tax on cement has been reduced from 12 per cent to 8 per cent. The government has announced a guarantee cover of 50 per cent of loans between Rs. 50 lakhs to Rs. 1 Crore for small and medium enterprises. The lock in period for loans covered under existing schemes will be reduced from 24 months to 18 months to encourage banks to cover more loans under the scheme.

The government announced another package of Rs. 35,000 Crores just within one month to bail out Indian Economy. The new package included the following:

1. The Reserve Bank of India cut the repo rate from 6.5 per cent to 5.5 per cent and reduced the cash reserve ratio (CRR) from 5.5 per cent to 5.0 per cent, to boost investment, spending and revive growth.
2. The reality companies have been allowed to borrow from overseas to develop "integrated townships".
3. Drawback benefits have been enhanced for some exporters. Export-import bank has also to get Rs. 5,000 Crores as credit from the Reserve Bank of India to revive exports.
4. Public Sector India Infrastructure Finance Company (IIFC) have been allowed to borrow Rs. 30,000 Crores from the market by issuing tax free bonds.
5. The Depreciation benefit on commercial vehicles has been increased from 15 per cent to 50 per cent on purchases, in order to stimulate the Commercial Vehicle Sector.
6. Ceiling on foreign institutional investments in corporate bonds has been increased to $ 15 billion from $ 6 billion to seek much bigger foreign institutional investment.

Again, on February 24, 2009, the government announced a slashing down of excise duty from 10 per cent to 8 per cent. Since, 90 per cent of the manufactured items attract 10 per cent of excise duty. This measure was intended to reduce the price of colour TV sets, Washing Machines, refrigerators, soaps.coolers, cars and commercial vehicles. Cement prices are likely to drop by (Rs. 4 Rs. 5) per bag of 50 kg bag. The steel prices may cost Rs. (500-600) per Tonne less. In addition to this the government also reduced the service tax from 12 per cent to 10 per cent. A reduction of 2 per cent in the service tax, will directly touch the lives of 500 million middle class families and will reduce their monthly expenses.

The entire stimulus package of Rs. 30,000 Crores was announced to boost demand in the economy and thus to reduce the impact of recession. On February 26, 2009, Commerce and Industry Minister announced a small relief package of Rs. 325 Crores for leather, textiles, Gems, and Jewellery.

Conclusion

The global financial crisis had a minimal effect on Indian Economy. The credit must go to India's approach to financial globalisation. The opening up current account convertibility, and full convertibility on capital account, the key regulatory bodies—RBI and SEBI keep a strong vigil on the activities of financial intermediaries. Unlike the advanced capitalistic countries like U.S.A., U.K. and European countries India has certain advantages. The high rate of savings, protected monetary sector and high rate of growth, growing information technology industry, Unexploited rural market, retail market economy, tourism sector, availability of cheap labour are the sliver line of success. The current survival agenda with particular focus on augmenting domestic demand and inclusive growth will energise the rural sector, encourage exports, and will enable sustainable development. The present steps taken for infrastructural development and rural employment will generate more employment and income. With the inflation regulated, the stimulus agenda will open the broad channel for robust growth. However, the leadership of steering the economy should not be left to the free market forces. Rather the government must regulate all sectors in order to promote balanced growth free from serious dislocation, from international and domestic forces.

REFERENCES

1. Keyness, J.M—The General Theory of Employment, MacMilan & Co. Ltd.
2. Reserve Bank of India 2007-08, Annual Reports. Monthly Bulletin September 2009.
3. Economic Survey, Govt of India 2008-09, Oxford University Press, New Delhi.
4. IMF(2008) World Economic Outlook Updates 6th Nov 2008 and 28th January 2009.
5. Securities and Exchange Board of India, (SEBI), Mumbai
6. 92nd Conference Volume 2009, Part-I of the Indian Economic Association, Patna.

CHAPTER 13

Global Thrust on SMEs
Ensuring Competitive Advantage

—DR. S.K. CHAUDHURY,
—DR. P.C. MAHAPATRA,
—PROF. K.R. SWAIN

Keywords

SMEs, SIDO, GDP, IMD, Wealth Creation, Global opportunities, Global thrust, Competative advantage, Enterpreneurial skills, free law, job creation, RTCs, SISIs, FTSs.

Introduction

There is a growing recognition worldwide that small and medium enterprises (SMEs) have an important role to play in the present context given their greater resource—use efficiency, capacity for employment generation, technological innovation, promoting inter-sectoral linkages, raising exports and developing entrepreneurial skills. Their locational flexibility is an important advantage in reducing regional imbalances. The future of SMEs is of major policy concern given their strategic importance in any discussion of reshaping the industrial sector. This is more so in the case of India, which has one of the longest histories of government support to the small-scale industrial sector since independence compared to most developing countries. In today's global economic scenario, establishing benchmarks at regional or national levels is not enough. These days, Indian SMEs need to benchmark their business process and relevant technologies as per global standards. Adoption of innovative ideas can, in effect, help in outclassing benchmarks, and in establishing new standards. Moreover, a culture of collaboration can increase the efficiencies of SMES and SSIs, and help them compare with established corporate. The small scale industries are viewed as an important vehicle for meeting both the growth and equity objectives of developing economies. The last two decades have witnessed the steady re- emergence of small scale Industries in both industrialised as well as industrialising countries, reducing the importance of economies of scale in mass production. Although correlation between the size of the industry and stage of industrialisation is not universal, the growth and expansion of small scale industrial sector have a positive impact on the rate of industrialisation in developing countries.

The present paper attempts to focus on the following aspects of SMEs :

- Various promotional measures for SMEs through institutional supports at international levels;
- Global contributions of SMEs, particularly in developed countries in terms of their share in employment and manufacturing sector;
- SMEs in Indian perspective with SWOT analysis; and
- Challenges before SMES for growth and barriers to sustainability.

Promotional Measures

Various low cost global assistance programs are available to help SMEs take advantage of global opportunities; state assistance, federal government assistance, and foreign assistance.

State Assistance: State assistance includes international marketing division (IMDs); worldwide network of world trade centers; chambers of commerce in foreign countries :

international business associations; international banks; and other such organizations. IMDs serve many foreign incoming and domestic outbound SMEs. Exhibit-I shows examples of information requests made of IMDs and Exhibit-II shows topics on which IMDs provide in – house and on- site counseling.

Exhibit—I : Examples of IMD Inquiries

Foreign Trade Zones, Industrial Property Tax Exemption Programmes Enterprise Zone Programmes, Inventory Tax Credit Programs Quick start Training Programme, Workforce Development and Training Programme, Capital Investment Tax Credit, Programme, Free Law Financial Service Center Banks.

Source : www.tded.state.la.us/new/intimktg/lang/English

Exhibit—II : Topic of IMD Counsel

How to identify international markets, Market research techniques, Sources of international trade data, Methods of export transactions, International trade terms, Methods of payment Modes of transportation.

Source : www.state.de.us/dedo/departments/trade/intntl.htm.

Trade shows and exhibits are important events permitting a state's business to get their product or service in front of global customers at reduced cost both space and provide these same companies hands-on, in country assistance.

Federal Government Assistance: The US Department of commerce offers assistance to US companies and associations attempting to expend beyond US borders. The American Chamber of Commerce provides exporting services, briefings on market conditions, and export/important trade leads. US embassies play a key role in arranging pre-screened and pre qualified leads.

Foreign Assistance: Many foreign countries seek foreign investments to bring vitality to their troubled economies. For example, Korea Trade Investment Promotion Agency has created a specialised division with the objective of providing a one stop investment center to help foreigners seeking investment center to help foreigners seeking investment opportunities in Korea. Other countries create trade centers around the world for the promotion of their countries investment opportunities.

Small firms rate the provision of foreign market information as the most important single service that government agencies can provide. The basic problems include :

1. That although the necessary information and support services are there, the governments "reactive" stance results in a lack of communication with SMEs that may not have the expertise or understanding to formulate a specific inquiry;
2. The concern that government speakers do not address the potential problems faced by SMEs in the early stage of export development; and
3. That SMEs have to lose day long productivity to take advantage of the currently offered day long seminars offered by many government agencies.

SMEs Contribution to the Global Environment

There is growing global appreciation of the fact that SMEs play an important role in the development of most economies. This fact is reflected in the form of their increasing number and rising proportion in the overall product manufacturing, exports, employment, technical innovations and promotion of entrepreneurial skills. The main policy interest in SME globalisation has to do with ways to create a net economic benefit, which usually means increasing sustainable job and wealth creation. SMEs can only create jobs and wealth by seking opportunities and by being efficient at taking advantage of them when they arise that has been reflected in fig 13.1. The following table reflects the contribution of SMEs in some of the developed economies.

Table 13.1. Contribution of SMEs in Some of the Developed Countries

Country	Contribution in terms of incremental share in	
	Employment	Manufacturing sector output
USA	67%	61%
Japan	80%	72%
France	53%	80%
Korea	74%	61%

(**Source:** Various issues of Business World & IVCA Reports)

	+ Creation	+ Expansion
New Job Creation		+ Birth
		– Death
	– Destruction	– Contraction
		Σ = not jobs created or lost

(**Source** : *OECD*)

Fig. 13.1. SMEs Job and Wealth Creation

Internationlisation opens up a greater range of opportunities for SMEs and thus increase their potential to contribute to economic well being [fig. 13.2].

Pool of SMEs in country A		Pool of opportunities in country A
Pool of SMEs in country B		Pool of opportunities in country B
Pool of SMEs in country C		Pool of opportunities in country C
Pool of globalised SMES		Global opportunities

(**Source** : OECD)

Fig 13.2. SMES and International Opportunities

SMEs in Indian Perspective

Importance of SMEs in India has been felt ever since it got its indepence. At present SMEs contributes 8 per cent of the GDP as well as provides employment to forty million people and it account for about forty five per cent of total exports.

National Level Institutional Support

The Ministry of Small Scale Industries, Government of India, designs policies, programmes, projects and schemes, and monitors implementation with a view to assisting the promotion and growth of small-scale industries.

Development Commission (Small Scale Industries) also known as Small Industries Development Organisation (SIDO) was established in 1954 on the basis of recommendation of the Ford Foundation. The aims and objectives of the organisation are to impart greater vitality and growth impetus to the small, tiny and village enterprises in terms of output, employment and exports and instilling a competitive culture based on heightened technology. Over 60 offices and 21 autonomous bodies are under its management. These autonomous bodies include tool rooms, training institutions and project-cum-process development centers. The facilities provided are-testing, training for entrepreneurship development, preparation of project and product profiles, technical and managerial consultancy, assistance for exports, pollution and energy audits etc. The role is of advocacy, hand-holding and facilitation for the small industries sector.

Globalisation of the Indian economy calls for small industries to reorient themselves to face new challenges. Recognising this changed environment SIDO is focussing on providing support in the fields of credit, marketing, technology and infrastructure to SSIs. The main services rendered are:

1. Advising the government in policy formulation for the promotion and development of small-scale industries.
2. Providing techno-economic and managerial consultancy, common facilities and extension services to small-scale units.
3. Providing facilities for technology up gradation, modernization, quality improvement and infrastructure.
4. Developing human resources through training and skill up gradation.
5. Providing economic information services.

6. Evolving and coordinating policies and programmes for development of Small Scale Industries as ancillaries to large and medium scale industries.
7. Monitoring of PMRY Scheme.

SIDO has a network of 30 Small Industries Service Institutes (SISIs), 28 Branch Small Industries Service Institute (SISIs), 4 Regional Testing Centers (RTCs), 7 Field Testing Stations (FTSs), 19 Autonomous Bodies which include 10 Tool Rooms (TRs) and Tool Design Institutes (TDI), 4 product-cum-process Development Centers (PPDCs), 2 Central Footwear Training Institute (CFTIs), 1 Electronic Service and Training Centre (ESTC), 1 Institute for Design of Electrical Measuring Instruments (IDEMI), 2 National Level Training Institutes, and 1 Departmental Training Institute and one Production centre.

SWOT Analysis of SMEs in India

Strengths	Weaknesses
• Contribution to National Economic Growth • Generating Employment and Vitalising India brand to the world • Regional Development • Technological Innovation • Export Market Expansion	• Lack of Funds. • Lack of marketing skill. • Lack of Information. • Poor adaptability to changing trade trends • Non- availability of technically trained human resources. • Lack of management skills. • Lack of access to technological information.
Opportunities	**Threats**
• WTO regime • Bilateral & multilateral trade agreements • Enhanced credit support • Support for technological upgradation. • Comprehensive support for cluster development. • Marketing assistance and export promotion support • Growing domestic and international markets.	• Dumping from developed countries. • Distrust between SMEs & Financial Institutions. • Poor incentive structures for entrepreneurs. • Virtual absence of enterprise Education. • Non-tariff barriers from developed countries. • Slow improvement in quality to meet the international standards.

Challenges to Small Firm Growth

For those firms main aim is growth, there are a number of challenges that have to be faced. In 1994, Churchill proposed a six-stage model for company growth. Each stage of the model is characterized by what Churchill describes as "an index of increasing size, complexity and / or dispersion ".

The model allows owners to assess the type of challenges facing them at current and future stages:

- Conception/existence
- Survival
- Profitability and stabilisation
- Profitability and growth
- Takeoff
- Maturity.

The model outlines expansion of customer base and increase in turnover as one of the key challenges faced in the conception/existence stage.

Sustainability and SMEs

In the United states, small business employ 50 per cent of the private work force and account for 52 per cent of the private sector input. While SMEs represent a primary source of economic development, they lag behind large corporation in the areas of environmental and social sustainability. Many SMEs face a variety of barriers to incorporate sustainability into their business practices, including.

- An inadequate understanding of the business case for sustainability.
- Lack of knowledge or required skills to integrate sustainability into their business strategy.
- Insufficient technology, expertise, training and capital to undertake sustainability initiatives in process development.

- Lack of awareness of the changing business environment due to a focus on the short term deliverables and the absence of strategic planning.
- Lack of sustainability tools tailored for small companies.
- Limited consumer or stakeholder pressure for the adoption of sustainable business practices.
- Lack of clarity in communication of sustainability expectations with customers, and external stakeholders, and
- Inadequate collaboration and decision making based on broad stakeholder input.

To facilitate the implementation of this strategy, the program sponsors conferences and workshops for SMEs and OEMs on why sustainability is becoming a business imperative, how their sustainability initiatives can be leveraged to gain a competitive supply chain advantage, and how to strategically plan and implement sustainability practices.

Conclusion

Governments need to take initiatives to ensure that the overall policy environment encourages industrial activity in general, and SME activity, in particular, given the latter's significant contribution to general economic activity in many countries. A number of steps have been initiated to promote the healthy growth of SSI sector. However, to ensure the prospects of these enterprises, SMEs, in the coming years will have to gear up to face the challenges of liberalisation SMEs have the remarkable prospect of competing successfully with established corporate houses by applying effective strategies that promote networking, collaborations and innovations.The key is to bring about a change in belief systems, which can be accomplished by public sector and private sector collaborations and developing their R&D infrastructure. The small scale units have been playing a very important role in our economy in terms of employment generation, export promotion and balanced regional development. The policies of liberalisation and de-reservation and openness have affected the growth pattern of this vital sector of our economy, particularly after 1993-94. The contribution of SME sector to the GDP in different countries is not on comparable parameters. Still, in both developed and developing economies, they were accorded special status, specific dispensations and particular attention. Although the broad canvas of 'enterprise' suggests that we look at the contribution of both industry and trade, more particularly exports, in the growth of GDP, lack of separate data on SME's contribution in the developed economies like the US, Canada, Japan and Germany restricted the scope of this paper to having a look at some policy interventions in ASEAN and OECD economies.

REFERENCES

1. Fact Sheet, 2002 *Press Information Bureau,* Government of India, New Delhi.
2. Perumalla, Dr. Vijaya, (2002), "Small–scale Industry Modernisation in India."
3. Economic Survey of India 1998-99.
4. Small Industries Development Organization Report, 2001 SIDO, Government of India.
5. Aiyer, S.S. Ankleshwar, (1997), "Create Small-scale Multinationals" *The Times of India,* March 23, 1997.
6. Papola, T.S., (2002), "Industry and Employment : Recent Indian Experience". Institute for Studies in Industrial Development, New Delhi.
7. Joshi, Vijaya and Little, IMD, (1998), *"India's Economic Reforms* 1991-2001" Oxford University Press, New Delhi.
8. Lingaiah K. and Satyanarayana T, (1990), *"Indian Economy"* Sterling Publishers (P) Ltd., New Delhi, 1990.
9. Rangarjan C. (2000), *"Perspectives on Indian Economy : A Collection of Essays"* UBSPD, New Delhi, 2000.
10. Business India, March 4, 2002, "The Growth and Transformation of Small Firms in India".

11. Highlights of EXIM Policy, 2002-07, Press Information Bureau, Government of India, New Delhi.
12. Year End Review (2002), "Special Package for Small Industries" Press Information Bureau, Govt. of India, New Delhi.
13. Datt R, and Sundharam KPM, (2003), "Indian Economy" S. Chand and Company Ltd, New Delhi, 2003.
14. Hornaday, J, Aboud, J (1971), "Characteristics of Successful Entrepreneurs", Personel Psychology, Vol. 24, pp. 141-53.
15. Rastogi, R. (2005), "The Reality of India", Aspects of India's Economy, No. 41.
16. Ruddardtt, KPM Sudaram, Indian Economy, 2000, S. Chand & Co., 2000.
17. Planning Commission. nic.in, Planning Commission Reports, Second Five Year Plan.
18. Annual Report on Small and Medium Industries 2005-06. Ministry of Small Scale Industries, Govt. of India.
19. Srinivasan, P. 2009. "Accounting and Revenue Recognition : Concerns of SMEs in India". *The Accounting World.* May 2009, pp. 14-21.

Index

H

S

T

U

V

W

Z

❑❑❑